TRAY TASKING

Activities that Promote Reading and Writing Readiness

Join us on the Web at

EarlyChildEd.delmar.com

TRAY TASKING

Activities that Promote Reading and Writing Readiness

Victoria Folds, Ed.D.

THOMSON

DELMAR LEARNING

Australia Canada Mexico Singapore Spain United Kingdom United States

Tray Tasking: Activities that Promote Reading and Writing Readiness
Victoria Folds, Ed.D.

Vice President, Career Education SBU:
Dawn Gerrain

Director of Editorial:
Sherry Gomoll

Acquisitions Editor:
Erin O'Connor

Editorial Assistant:
Stephanie Kelly

Director of Production:
Wendy A. Troeger

Production Editor:
Joy Kocsis

Production Assistant:
Angela Iula

Director of Marketing:
Wendy E. Mapstone

Cover Illustration:
Chris Watkins

Channel Manager:
Kristin McNary

Marketing Coordinator:
David White

Composition:
Larry O'Brien

Library of Congress Cataloging-in-Publication Data

Folds, Victoria.
  Tray tasking : activities that promote reading and writing readiness / Victoria Folds.
     p. cm.
  Includes bibliographical references and index.
  ISBN 1-4018-7226-3
  1. Language arts (Early childhood)--Activity programs.
  I. Title.
  LB1139.5.L35F65 2005
  372.6--dc22
                      2004023851

CONTENTS

CHAPTER 3 Wet Transfer Tray Tasking Activities   35

CHAPTER 4 Arranging Your Small Manipulatives and Math Center   61

CHAPTER 5 Preparing Your Language Center   73

Dedication

To my father and mother, Arthur and Betty Speaks, for their endless confidence and love, and to my husband Charlie and children Abbie, Jennifer, and Joshua, whose support and encouragement are greatly appreciated.

PREFACE

This book was written for early childhood teachers and families of young children. The purpose of the book is to provide new and innovative ways to engage young children in activities that promote whole body integration for reading and writing skills while having fun at the same time. Young children need opportunities to develop body coordination. Tray Tasking focuses on activities that promote coordinated large and fine motor movement using both sides of the body to reinforce the concepts of left to right and top to bottom directionalities.

Having been involved with young children for over 25 years, teaching, directing child care programs, being an adjunct professor of early childhood courses in both community and university settings, and writing curriculum, I have watched children's eagerness to attend to meaningful tasks when presented with interesting materials. I have studied the Montessori method during my years of formal education and believe in Montessori's thinking: that play is a child's work. I have observed as children worked with Montessori's Practical Life elements and felt that I could adapt into a more focused outcome toward reading and writing readiness.

HOW TRAY TASKING CAME TO BE

My original setting began with preschool and pre-kindergarten–level classrooms. I designed tray activities and displayed them on open shelving next to the Small Manipulatives area. I designated one table next to the shelves and labeled it the Tray Task Table. I would place a Tray Task at the table for children to investigate. I printed all the children's first names on a list and attached it to the table. I would explain to children at Circle Time about the new interest center and invite them to visit the area during child choice time. If a child wished to complete the activity, the child would check off his or her name and begin. I would observe each child attempting a Tray Task. This gave me a chance to observe whether the child crossed the midline, completed a task, and moved in a left to right direction and other traits. The findings would go into the child's portfolio where I listed all tray activities. I used a check mark for the satisfactory completion of a task, a "WTH" if the child completed "with teacher's help," and left the area blank if I wanted to provide another opportunity for the child to complete the task. These were especially helpful indicators of learning when discussing a child during a parent/teacher conference. The use of the tray charting in the portfolio showed concrete evidence of growth over time.

From these activities I began to create a list of activities that would reinforce the movements using a variety of household objects that would be familiar to young children. I looked for function, movable parts, sizing, flexibility, and construction. I gathered utensils, containers and other materials and organized a Tray Tasking Learning Center.

I have been presenting seminars at numerous workshops and conferences over the years and have always received a positive response about Tray

Tasking's overall application and purpose. Those responses encouraged me to write a book that can serve as a teacher resource for setting up a Tray Tasking area and that is filled with ideas to pique a child's curiosity through the use of simple, common items moved in specific ways.

There is no other teacher resource book available that details the significance of combining reading and writing readiness than *Tray Tasking*. *Tray Tasking* promotes these abilities by providing a "best practice" approach to today's most important abilities in a child's life combined with a child's innate willingness to make sense of the world through hands-on activities.

If an adult, whether it be teacher or family member, wishes to engage a child in a Tray Task, the only preparation needed is in the assembling of the task. I have observed teachers using a Tray Task and I could see the satisfaction on the teachers' faces as they watched a child accomplish the purpose of the Tray Task activity.

Tray Tasking provides families with real signs of learning without reverting to formal paper and pencil tasks.

HOW THE BOOK IS ORGANIZED

Chapter 1 provides insight as to several foundational influences. Montessori and Piaget are cited in connection to the ideas in this book. A background on the importance of whole body bilateral integration is provided as well as ways to identify handedness. The direct correlation of the suggested activities and reading and writing outcomes becomes clear as you begin to implement the Tray Tasking activities.

Chapter 2 lists Tray Tasking activities that are dry in their application. This means there is no use of water in any of these selections.

Chapter 3 provides activities using water, which are referred to as wet transfer Tray Tasking activities. I suggest that these activities be placed in a tiled area of the classroom.

The next chapters offer ideas for different learning centers in your classroom. Take a moment and look at your interest centers. Use the following suggested guidelines for your classroom:

1. Follow the three A's:
   a. All materials should be *accessible*.
   b. All materials should be *available*.
   c. All materials should be *attractive*.

2. Separate multipiece activities into tasks.

3. The use of color-coordinated baskets and trays help a child learn that there is a place for everything and everything has a place.

4. Label all learning activities with pictures and words.

5. Supplement your interest centers with new or extended activities as you see children's interests change, usually every six to eight weeks.

By adapting Tray Tasking techniques, you can

- extend the number of child choices in the classroom.
- focus on skill building with each child.
- encourage children to be independent learners.
- create manageable challenges that engage children's curiosity.
- build self-esteem.

Chapter 4 provides activities and ideas for your Small Manipulative and Math Learning Center. You can extend your current learning equipment in this area by arranging many of them into Tray Tasks.

Chapter 5 encourages you to look at your Language Learning Center through new eyes with suggested activities that capture the reading and writing elements into your learning center.

Chapter 6 touches on the Science Learning Center with activities for displaying items using readiness skills.

Chapter 7 encourages involvement with families by using a Tray Tasking Observation Chart.

The display and maintenance of Tray Tasks should follow the guidelines just given. The materials on each tray are never to be used in any other activity, moved or combined with other learning center materials. Tray Tasking materials are specific to the task they are intended. Before displaying, you should demonstrate the Tray Task during a Circle Time gathering and share your excitement about these special tasks. Children will appreciate the time and effort taken to prepare the materials. Explain to them that you expect them to take good care of the materials so that everyone can enjoy them.

I have found that many times an agitated child will calm down when engaged in a Tray Task. A child may slow down his or her breathing and body actions while completing a Tray Task and thus increase concentration and successful completion of a task.

ACKNOWLEDGMENTS

The author wishes to thank Charlie Folds for his phenomenal photo skills, and the staff at the First Presbyterian Preschool, for letting us shoot pictures. A special thanks to Cheryl Stone, Center Director.

A special thank you is also given to Marilou Raham, owner of Children's World, for her permission to shoot pictures at her center.

I would also like to express gratitude to Alexis Breen Ferraro and Ivy Ip whose guidance and support have been appreciated.

The editors at Thomson Delmar Learning and the author thank the following reviewers for their time, effort, and thoughtful contributions that helped to shape the final text.

Wendy Bertoli, M.Ed.
Lancaster County Career and Center for
   Technology
Lancaster, PA

Patricia Capistron
Rocking Unicorn Preschool
Harwich, MA

Linda Estes, Ed.D.
St. Charles Community College
St. Peters, MO

Heather Fay
Early Childhood Educator
Akron, OH

Catherine Henris
Active Learning Center
Franklin, TN

Sandra Hughes
Rainbow Express Child Care Center
Schenectady, NY

Karen Manning
Child Care Consultant
Schenectady, NY

Jody Martin
Crème de la Crème
Aurora, CO

Sandy Wlaschin
University of Nebraska at Omaha Child Care
   Center
Omaha, NE

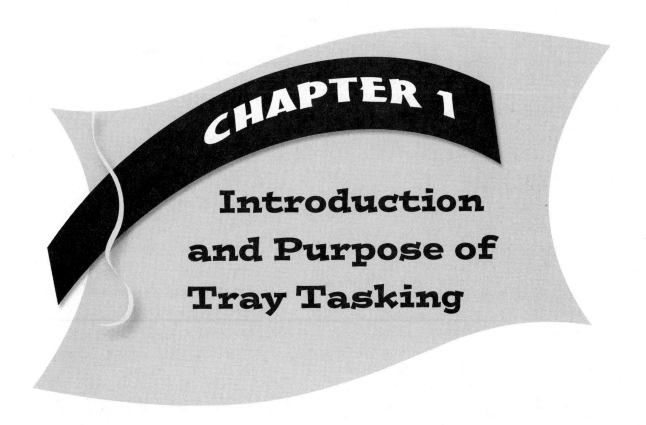

CHAPTER 1

Introduction and Purpose of Tray Tasking

MARIA MONTESSORI'S INFLUENCE

Maria Montessori (1870–1952) was an important early childhood educator who provided guidance in the notion of utilizing familiar household objects organized with a learning outcome. Dr. Montessori believed that a valid impulse to learning is the self-motivation of the child. Children move themselves toward learning. This book acts upon that theory by developing Tray Tasks. Children are drawn to individual lessons that offer a preplanned learning outcome. The teacher can then act as a facilitator of the learning process. It is the child who is motivated through the task itself to persist until completion.

Dr. Montessori felt that children are free to learn when they task their inner discipline to want to learn. Through Tray Tasking, a child establishes and perpetuates concentration, determination, and thoroughness, which produces a self-confident, competent learner in later years.

Tray Tasking permits a teacher to teach little but observe much. We can generate guidelines through Montessori teachings that still apply today:

1. Observation is the first role of the teacher.
   a. Perceive the needs of the child.
   b. Observe the child objectively in order to determine the best approach.
   c. Observe the effectiveness of the environment in relation to the child.
   d. Observe interactions among children.

2. We are all observers and should
   a. act as the observer and initiator rather than the intruder.
   b. not interrupt a child's attempt, rather observe the outcomes.
   c. remain calm and open-minded.
   d. observe as if all attempts are to be regarded as important indicators.

3. Appropriate approaches to observation:
   a. When observing a child, do not speak loudly or interact with another adult within child's hearing and seeing range.
   b. Observe in such a way as to not cause a child to become nervous.
   c. "Observing while walking" is a teacher technique that should be employed.

Tray Tasking provides an opportunity for observation to occur. When children engage in Tray Tasking, the adult can actually see the child strengthening grasp control, focusing on his or her ability to coordinate movement, and discovering his or her ability to complete a task.

PIAGET'S INFLUENCE

Jean Piaget's (1897–1980) cognitively based theory provided another influence for writing *Tray Tasking*. Piaget contends that a child learns new knowledge every day and builds upon that knowledge depending on the learning environment and how he or she applies the new knowledge to learning situations. Piaget referred to the learning of new knowledge as "assimilating" and how the child uses that knowledge as "accommodating." These actions are observed through Tray Tasking. As a child acts upon the environment, he or she revisits existing information and adds the new piece of information in the brain. Thus, the child is accommodating new information that creates a new level of knowledge about a particular learning episode. For example, yesterday Johnny selected a Tray Tasking activity to complete. He investigated the materials, and its purpose, transferring water from the left to the right bowl. He attempted to pick up the transfer tool and move the water from one bowl to another. Today, he approaches the Tray Task with more confidence, with a memory of having used the materials. His ability to control the transfer tool, increase his attention span, and complete the task is met with more satisfaction. The child reaches what Piaget referred to as "equilibration." The child has balanced his or her assimilating and accommodating abilities as part of a self-regulatory mechanism necessary to ensure the development of his interaction within the environment. This process happens all the time when a child is discovering and learning new knowledge. Thus, from birth throughout life, knowledge is said to be continually constructed by individuals in a perpetual quest for learning.

BILATERAL COORDINATION

Bilateral coordination means the ability of a child to use both sides of the body in harmony to produce meaningful outcomes. Tray Tasking promotes the use of bilateral coordination through the use of eye tracking and arm and hand movements as well as motions that cross the midline. The midline is an imaginary line from head to toe that separates the body into two halves. It is used as a reference tool when discussing the body's ability to coordinate movement successfully.

Children may have difficulty with bilateral integration because they have not had exposure to many activities that promote the function. The lack of bilateral coordination opportunities may result in the following:

1. difficulty coordinating two sides of the body
2. Possible right and left confusion
3. Avoidance of crossing the midline of the body
4. Lack of hand dominance
5. Difficulty with projected action sequences such as tossing an object to a target

HANDEDNESS AND BRAIN LINKAGE

Midline activities encourage communication between the two sides of the brain. When the two sides of the body fail to integrate their functions, there is usually a tendency to avoid crossing the body's midline. This may result in each hand preferring to operate on its own side of the body. This practice interferes with the normal development of a preferred hand for skilled work. Hand dominance encourages one side of the brain to be dominating, which is necessary for more difficult motor tasks. The brain is at its greatest efficiency when the hemispheres are working together utilizing specific functions.

Research tells us that there are two distinct parts to the brain, usually referred to as the left and right hemispheres. However, there is a little known bridge that connects the two sides so that bilateral integration of information occurs. It is called the corpus callosum, a thick stretch of neural tissue in the middle of the brain that connects and conveys information. The callosum takes on an active role from infancy in directing the development of the brain into the highly lateralized organ it becomes. The function of the corpus callosum during cognitive activity seems to be one of maintaining the balance of attention between the two sides that enables each side to contribute its part to achieve an integrated whole. It also allocates different kinds of processing to the area of the brain that is programmed for the distribution of attention over the two hemispheres and enables sustained attention during complex cognitive tasks.

HOW TRAY TASKING RELATES TO READING AND WRITING

Tray Tasking provides young children with the challenge of using common every day household materials organized in such a way as to promote whole body coordination refinement. This book moves a child's body motions through top to bottom and left to right directions; the same universal directions needed for formal reading and writing acquisition. Young children need opportunities to engage the whole body in activities that help center the child's coordination. Gross and fine motor activities that promote coordinated movement from both sides of the body reinforce the skills necessary for life-long learning.

Traditionally, many think of reading and writing activities only as paper and pencil tasks. Families also relate printed materials that come home with a child as a child's "work." Teachers who work with young children have the responsibility of educating families about alternative, effective means to convey that reading and writing readiness is occurring every day in many ways.

Young children are active learners. Their whole bodies need to move to rhythm and music and movement experiences that stabilize balance and encourage flexibility, coordination, and centering. Every item in a classroom is a reading and writing activity. From doll washing to bead stringing, we can validate the actions, movements, and outcomes as readiness related.

Tangible examples of learning occur through the use of Tray Tasking. A Tray Tasking learning center might be established as a stand-alone area or an extension of the Sensory or Fine Motor areas. Tray Tasking materials are specifically arranged so that a child engages in reading and writing movements as a by-product while completing a fun Tray Task.

By definition I describe a Tray Task as a prepared hands-on activity that promotes reading and writing readiness skills utilizing common household items arranged on a tray. The purpose of a Tray Task is to promote lateral movement of eyes and coordinate arms and hands in harmony to effect an outcome of left to right and top to bottom movements. These movements are key elements in future formal reading and writing activities. To build typical tray-tasking lessons, begin with basic equipment such as a tray, items strategically placed on a tray, and an appliance for transferring material from one location to another.

Many early childhood pioneers in education point out that young children learn by doing. Tray Tasking provides the actions and movements necessary for young children's bodies and minds to get ready for more formal education.

Four ways Tray Tasking activities contribute to reading and writing readiness are:

1. crossing the body midline with one or both arms

2. eye tracking from left to right and top to bottom

3. refinement of muscle strength

4. logical consequences of a beginning, middle, and end of a task

The strengths of Tray Tasking are in the concepts. They

1. provide easy-to-assemble elements within the environment that concentrate the child's efforts toward learning outcomes.

2. provide inexpensive ways to expand hands-on learning materials in the classroom.

3. provide a child with a comfort level of familiar materials to be used in a new way.

4. establish a Tray Tasking learning center in the classroom where children may choose from an assortment of challenges.

Tray Tasking is organized in an alphabetic format. Each activity can be used independently. Each Tray Task provides one page of information and a picture showing the placement of the materials. The information follows a format of listing materials, setup, task, and outcome along with the readiness skill to be achieved. Safety hints are also provided for many of the activities.

It is recommended that Tray Tasking be part of the child-choice center learning times during the preschool classroom day. Teachers can introduce Tray Tasking at Circle Time and place demonstrated Tray Tasks on shelves. Tray Tasking is not intended to be a large group activity where every child is completing a Tray Task at the same time. Children who are interested in completing the activity individually choose Tray Tasks.

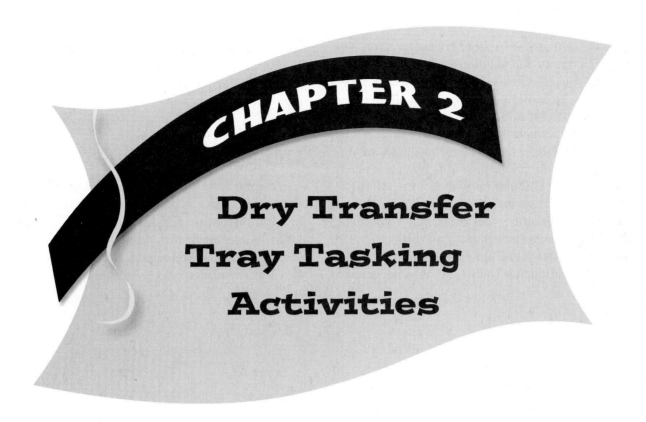

CHAPTER 2

Dry Transfer Tray Tasking Activities

INTRODUCTION

Dry transfer Tray Tasking involves using materials such as rice, grains, paper, and items that are dry in nature. Dry transfer Tray Tasks present a challenge to young children as they work with materials that move, pour, separate, and group together.

AGE RANGE RECOMMENDATION

The dry transfer Tray Tasks are written for preschool age children who are no more than two years from kindergarten entrance. *Tray Tasking* is written for the older three-, four-, and five-year-old preschool child.

HEALTH AND SAFETY ISSUES

You are the best monitor of selecting the appropriate size and texture of dry materials to be used when creating each Tray Task. The choking rule of "learning equipment should be bigger than your thumb" may not apply in such cases as when using rice, cornmeal, confetti, or similar sized items. You are to select materials that you feel will not pose a health or safety issue for your children. Please substitute when you feel that it is appropriate so that the Tray Task provides the same element of concentration, learning outcome, and challenge for your children.

Always check your allergy list when selecting ingredients for dry transfer Tray Tasks.

DISPLAY IDEAS

A recommended way to display the dry transfer Tray Tasks is individually, on open shelving units. Each task should have the complete materials on its tray. This means you need to regularly check that enough grain, rice, and the like, is available for each activity and that you have replenished what is needed. The best time to do that is at the end of each day.

Use sentence strip paper to label each tray area and each tray so that children replace a Tray Task to its proper shelf. Labeling provides another print-rich learning experience for your children and relates to the rest of the learning classroom where print-rich experiences are apparent.

The learning center where Tray Tasks are displayed can be a separate area with tables and chairs nearby or in combination with a Small Motor or Small Manipulative area. Do not combine Tray Tasks on shelves with other types of learning equipment. Tray Tasks should be separate and distinct so that children respect and appreciate their value. After gradually introducing each Tray Task and demon-strating their use during circle times over the course of several weeks, you should end up with at least ten displayed Tray Tasks that are always available for children's choices.

STORAGE IDEAS

A recommended way to store extra materials for future Tray Tasks is in plastic bins. Plastic bags should be used to hold your transfer textures and store at room temperature, away from the children. Label each baggie so that you can readily replenish or create new Tray Tasks. Keep bags away from children's reach.

Bead Tray Task

✎ Materials

- ✘ one plastic rectangular tray
- ✘ one lacing string
- ✘ one small bowl
- ✘ five to seven beads
- ✘ one visual instruction card for sequencing of beads (store bought or teacher made)

✎ Setup

1. Place tray in a horizontal position.
2. Place lacing string across top of tray in horizontal direction.
3. Place beads in small bowl in the middle of the tray.
4. Attach visual instruction card along bottom of tray.

✎ Task

The goal is for the child to lace beads on the lacing string according to the instructional card. The child should select one bead at a time and string it on the lace following the colors and/or shapes of the beads shown on the card. A card may be in color or in black and white. A black-and-white card encourages shape-only stringing, whereas the colored card suggests stringing by color.

✎ Outcome

After stringing is completed, ask the child to place the beads below the card so that they match. This activity is self-checking. The child should be able to decide whether beads are in the correct order.

When the child shows you his or her completed work, ask the following question: "Can you read me your beads?" The child may respond by using the color codes or the shapes in describing the

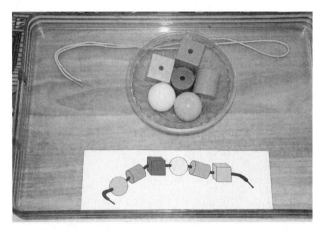

Used by permission of Learning Resources

beads. Thus, a child might "read" blue, red, green, orange, and yellow. Or, a child might "read" square, triangle, square, rectangle, circle.

✎ Readiness Skills

This activity encourages a child to assign a meaning to the materials as practice for reading. The action strengthens finger muscles for writing skills as well as encourages left to right visual discrimination.

✎ Safety Hint

Wooden beads can be a choking hazard. When demonstrating this activity, be sure to talk about how we handle beads with hands only and keep beads on the tray.

✎ Teacher Tip

Many stringing bead sets come with sentence strip cards that show beads in a certain order by color or by shape. You can make these by using sentence strips and drawing five to seven beads in a row by color, shape, and/or size. A child will use this as a guide to string the beads in that order.

Buckle Tray Task

 ## Materials

- one plastic rectangular tray
- a frame with buckle belt or a stuffed doll with buckled belt

 ## Setup

1. Place tray in a vertical position.
2. Place frame or doll vertically on tray.

 ## Task

The child is to buckle, using both hands.

 ## Outcome

The goal of this activity is to strengthen finger control and eye tracking as the child uses both hands to handle and fasten a buckle.

A child can transfer this skill to buckling other belts, shoes, and items in the classroom such as dramatic play clothes.

 ## Readiness Skills

By engaging in this Tray Task, a child is strengthening his or her eye-hand coordination, midline focus, small muscle control, and eye tracking.

 ## Teacher Tip

A common source for buckling may be a doll dressed with an outfit with buckles. Or, you can use belts with buckles and place them around a stuffed doll or attach to an empty picture frame.

Cloth Napkin Folding Tray Task

Materials

- one plastic rectangular tray
- one cloth napkin in a solid, bright color

Setup

1. Place tray in a horizontal position.
2. Place one cloth napkin, opened, in a horizontal position.

Task

The child is to practice folding using two directions: top to bottom and left to right.

Upon completion, the child will have folded the napkin twice.

Outcome

The teacher should observe corner-to-corner placement as well as the ability of the child to complete a task following a two-step instruction.

Readiness Skills

Napkin folding encourages a child to cross the midline and use coordinated movements to achieve a goal.

Clothes Folding Tray Task

Materials

- ✖ one plastic rectangular tray
- ✖ one small suitcase with zipper or clasp for opening and closing
- ✖ several clothing items, such as T-shirt and shorts
- ✖ one small clothes bin (or lay clothes to side of tray)

Setup

1. Place tray in vertical position.
2. Place clothes bin to the left of the tray.
3. Place suitcase to the right of the tray.

Task

- ■ Encourage child to remove one item of clothing from the clothes bin.
- ■ Place item on tray for folding activity.
- ■ Practice top to bottom, left to right folding.
- ■ Place folded item in suitcase.

Outcome

Child successfully folds clothes and places them in suitcase.

Readiness Skills

Increases use of both hands in coordinated manner. Encourages the following of directions and completing a task.

Clothespin and Clothesline Tray Task

 ## Materials

- one plastic rectangular tray
- one section of clothesline
- 10 plastic or wooden clothespins (spring type)
- one small bowl

 ## Setup

1. Place tray in a horizontal position.
2. Place clothespins in a bowl to the left of the tray.
3. Place clothesline across the middle of the tray.

Task

Child is to select one clothespin at a time and clip onto the clothesline until all ten clothespins are on the rope in a row.

 ## Outcome

The goal is to pinch each clothespin and clip onto the clothesline.

 ## Readiness Skills

By completing this task, the child practices the pincer movement, which increases the finger dexterity needed to hold a pencil. It also promotes eye-hand coordination and increases concentration.

 ## Safety Hint

Use plastic or wooden spring–type clothespins. Encourage the children to practice opening and pinching clothespins so that the children do not pinch fingers.

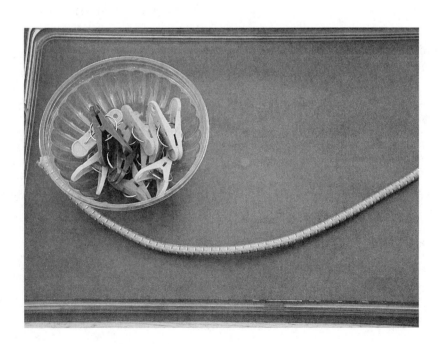

Cornmeal and Rice Sifter Tray Task

 Materials

- ✖ one plastic rectangular tray
- ✖ one plastic 1-cup measuring cup ½ filled with rice
- ✖ one plastic 1-cup measuring cup ½ filled with cornmeal
- ✖ one handheld flour sifter
- ✖ one bowl

 Setup

1. Place bowl in middle of tray.
2. Place both measuring cups to the left of the tray.
3. Place sifter to right of tray.

Task

- ■ Child rests sifter inside of bowl.
- ■ Child pours rice into sifter.
- ■ Child pours cornmeal into sifter and squeezes sifter handle and holds slightly above bowl while sifting ingredients into bowl.

 Outcome

As child is sifting, ask the child "What is happening to the rice?" "Do both ingredients go through the sifter?" "Why or why not?" Child is learning that not all ingredients sift. When completed, pour sifter

of rice back into measuring cup. Pour bowl contents of cornmeal back into measuring cup. Ready the activity for another child.

 Readiness Skills

This is a good activity for eye-hand coordination. Child is working on strengthening grasp control, which will parallel pencil holding. Child is completing a task using several steps. Child is working on handedness when holding sifter.

 Safety Hint

When demonstrating this activity, talk about how we keep the rice and cornmeal on the tray.

Dry Pouring Tray Task

 Materials

- ✘ one plastic rectangular tray
- ✘ two 2-cup measuring cups with spouts and handles
- ✘ colored sand or colored rice

 Setup

1. Arrange two measuring cups side by side in middle of horizontal tray.
2. The cup on the left should be ½ filled with pouring grain.

 Task

- ■ Child is to pour from one measuring cup into the other.

- ■ Child is not to spill sand or rice on the tray.
- ■ When completed, pour right measuring cup back into left one.

 Outcome

Child will successfully pour sand or rice from the left container to the right container.

 Readiness Skills

Causes child to cross the midline, coordinate body movements using hands, arms, and eyes.

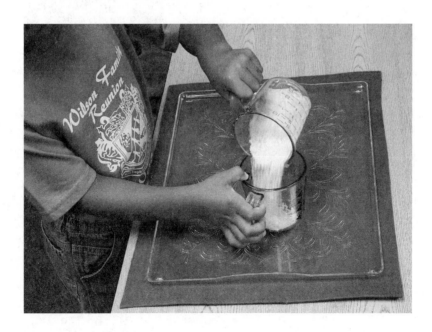

Flower Arranging Tray Task

Materials

- one plastic rectangular tray
- three plastic flower vases
- six plastic flowers (three pairs)

Setup

1. Place plastic flower vases on tray in a row.
2. Place flowers across top of tray.

Task

Ask child to place flowers in each vase, one at a time.

Outcome

- Child will decide which flowers go into which vases.
- Teacher will observe whether child divides flowers into two flowers per vase by matching colors or types or places one in the first vase, two in the second vase, and three in the third vase. All decisions are viewed as successful.

Readiness Skills

Child crosses the midline, coordinates body actions and eyes.

Hole Punch Tray Task

 ## Materials

- one plastic rectangular tray
- one single hole paper punch
- two plastic transparent bowls
- scraps of colored construction paper

 ## Setup

1. Place first bowl on left of tray filled with paper scraps.
2. Place second empty bowl next to the first bowl.
3. Lay paper punch across top of tray.

 ## Task

- Child picks up one scrap of paper, holds over bowl, and hole punches into bowl.
- Child continues until all paper is used.

 ## Outcome

Child successfully punches holes.

 ## Readiness Skills

- promotes the use of both hands with eye-hand coordination
- multitasking by holding and punching at the same time
- promotes hand-grasping and handedness strengthening

 ## Safety Hint

Single hole punches may also be found in the Creative Art or Small Motor sections of your classroom. Talk about what should and should not be used with a hole punch.

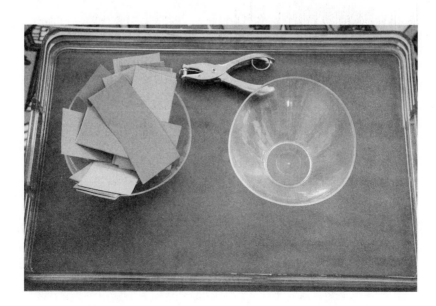

Lacing Tray Task

 ## Materials

- ✖ one plastic rectangular tray
- ✖ one frame or large shoe
- ✖ laces attached to frame or shoelaces for shoes

 ## Setup

1. If using frame, place in middle of tray.

2. If using shoe, lace it in middle of tray with toe of shoe at top of tray in vertical direction.

3. Use shoelaces that are distinct in color. Knot two different solid colors and secure the lacing so that the knot is in the middle of the first eyes.

 ## Task

Encourage child to complete the lacing from top of the frame or shoe to the bottom. By using two different colors, the child can see how the lacing travels in and out of the eyes.

 ## Outcome

Child completes lacing.

 ## Readiness Skills

As the child begins to hold and lace the shoe, he or she is crossing the midline. The child is strengthening eye-hand coordination and fine muscles.

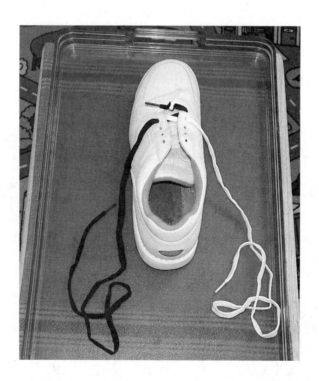

Ladle and Rice Tray Task

 ## Materials

 one plastic rectangular tray

✘ one large spoon or ladle

✘ two bowls (can be same color as the ladle or transparent)

Setup

1. Place tray in a horizontal position.
2. Place two bowls side by side forming left to right row.
3. Place ladle above bowls, lengthwise.
4. Place ½ cup colored rice in first (left) bowl.

Task

■ Child is to transfer the rice from the left bowl to the right bowl.

■ Ask child to pick up the ladle or spoon (observe handedness).

 ■ Encourage child to scoop ladle into first bowl and transfer the rice to the second bowl. Dip or scoop as many times as necessary so that the first bowl is empty and the second bowl is filled with rice.

Outcome

The goal is to successfully transfer the rice from the left bowl to the right bowl without spilling any rice onto the tray or table.

Readiness Skills

While completing this task, the child is moving the body from a left to right direction, which is the same direction needed for reading. The child is also moving hands and arms in the left to right direction necessary for writing.

Large Button Tray Task

Materials

- ✘ one plastic rectangular tray
- ✘ one frame or doll with buttons on the outfit

Setup

1. Place tray in a vertical position.
2. Place frame or doll on tray.

Task

- Child is to button each buttonhole by placing the button into the hole.

- Encourage child to begin at the top buttonhole and move down the doll.

Outcome

The goal of this Tray Task is for the child to successfully button each hole.

Readiness Skills

This Tray Task increases the child's ability to use his or her fingers in a defined, coordinated direction. These same skills are necessary for grasping and holding a pencil.

Mortar and Pestle Tray Task

Materials

- one plastic rectangular or circular tray
- one mortar and pestle set
- several saltine crackers
- one small plastic bag

Setup

1. Place tray in horizontal position or center of workspace.
2. Place mortar and pestle set on the tray with mortar to the left of the pestle.
3. Place a saltine cracker inside the pestle.

Task

- The child is to pick up the mortar (handle) with either hand and churn the cracker inside the bowl.

- Upon completion, child is to pour crumbs into plastic bag.

Outcome

The goal of this Tray Task is for the child to have practice in wrist turning while holding on to the mortar. This motion strengthens the wrist and hand muscles.

Readiness Skills

This Tray Task offers refinement in eye-hand coordination and muscle development, which are the essentials for reading and writing.

Safety Hint

One small plastic bag is all that is used for this activity. The bag never leaves the tray.

Paper Tearing Tray Task

Materials

✖ one plastic rectangular tray

✖ two containers (such as a bowl, shallow box, etc.)

✖ several 1-inch × 4-inch strips of colored construction paper

Setup

1. Place tray in horizontal position.

2. Place two containers side by side.

3. Place strips of colored paper into container on the left.

Task

■ Encourage child to select one strip of paper at a time and tear into squares.

■ Place the torn pieces of paper into the container on the right side of the tray.

Outcome

Child will complete the tearing of all strips of paper in the first container.

Readiness Skills

■ By tearing paper, the child uses muscles and coordinated movements that strengthen thumb and finger dexterity.

■ The task also causes the child to hold paper at the midline of the body, thus centering attention and focusing eyes and hand/arm movements toward the center of the body.

Teacher Tip

Save all torn paper and place in art area to be used for collage making.

Pom-Pom and Tong Tray Task

Materials

- one plastic rectangular tray
- two bowls (plastic and transparent)
- one safety tong
- ten large colored pom-poms

Setup

1. Place tray in a horizontal position.
2. Arrange two bowls side by side on tray.
3. Place safety tong above bowls.
4. Place colored pom-poms in first (left) bowl.

Task

- The task requires the child to pick up the safety tong and transfer the pom-poms from the left bowl to the right bowl.
- Encourage the child to transfer one at a time. An extension of this activity would be to place an activity card below the bowls and ask the child to transfer pom-poms by the colors on the card.

Outcome

The goal is for the child to successfully pinch each pom-pom with the safety tong and transfer one pom-pom at a time into the bowl to the right of the first bowl.

Readiness Skills

This task requires the use of crossing the midline, eye-hand coordination, grasping control, and coordinated movement from left to right. These are the same body skills necessary for future reading and writing movements.

Safety Hint

Choose only smooth edged tongs that are easy to open and close.

Sand and Shell Sift Tray Task

Materials

- ✘ one plastic rectangular tray
- ✘ one handheld flour sifter
- ✘ one bowl
- ✘ two 1-cup plastic measuring cups
- ✘ sand and small shells

Setup

1. Place tray in horizontal position.
2. Place two measuring cups one above the other on the left side of the tray.
3. Place flour sifter at top of tray.
4. Place bowl on the right side of tray.

Task

- The task requires the child to set the flour sifter inside the bowl and pour the cup containing sand and the cup containing small shells into the sifter.

- Then, the child is to slightly raise the flour sifter and sift into the bowl.
- Upon completion, the child is to pour sand back into a cup and place shells back into a cup.

Outcome

- The purpose of this Tray Task is for the child to observe that only the sand sifts through the sifter while the shells remain in the sifter.
- A discussion as to why this occurs is suggested.

Readiness Skills

- Grasping a flour sifter is a challenge.
- Observe how the child attempts to coordinate body balance and movement to accomplish this task.
- This task requires patience and attending to the task until completion.

Scoop and Beans Tray Task

 ## Materials

 one plastic rectangular tray

two bowls

one plastic scoop

one plastic measuring cup of large uncooked beans

 ## Setup

1. Place tray in horizontal position.
2. Place two bowls on tray side by side.
3. Place scoop across the top of the tray.
4. Place one cup of beans to the left of the first bowl.

Task

- Ask child to pour beans into the first bowl.
- Ask child to transfer beans from the left bowl to the right bowl using a plastic scoop.

 ## Outcome

The child will determine which hand he or she wishes to use to pick up the scoop. The child will attend to the task until completion.

 ## Readiness Skills

The child uses body movements that cross the midline, provide an opportunity to grasp a transfer tool, and complete a task from left to right.

 ## Safety Hints

- Select large beans.
- Do not use kidney beans or small chickpea beans.
- Talk about choking or inhaling hazards with your children and demonstrate that beans remain either in the bowl or transfer instrument at all times.

 ## Teacher Tip

Extend the Tray Tasking activity by asking child to transfer one bean at a time using his or her fingers and count how many beans are in the bowl.

Shape Sort Tray Task

Materials

- ✘ one plastic rectangular tray
- ✘ paper template of shapes in two rows of three shapes each
- ✘ six plastic or laminated paper shapes in various colors

Setup

1. Place tray in a horizontal position.
2. Secure paper template to the inside of the tray.
3. Place bowl of plastic or laminated paper shapes to the left of the tray.

Task

- ■ Ask child to select one shape at a time and place in the template beginning with the first row, first column.
- ■ Encourage child to complete both rows from left to right.

Outcome

This task requires a child to problem solve by placing shapes in the insets of the template.

Readiness Skills

The child is using the same eye and hand directions as reading or writing from left to right and top to bottom.

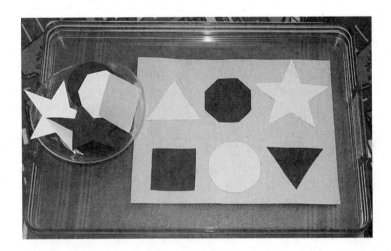

Size Sort Tray Task

 Materials

- one plastic rectangular tray
- paper template of various size and shape outlines in two rows of three each
- laminated paper or plastic shapes
- container for shapes

 Setup

1. Place tray in horizontal position.
2. Secure template to the inside of tray.
3. Place container for shapes to the left of the tray.

 Task

This task requires the child to select the shape to match the outline beginning with the first row, first column. Thereafter, the child selects the shape according to the template outline and places each shape until completed.

 Outcome

Upon completion, the child has completed a two-row, three-column template by matching various sizes of shapes to outlines.

 Readiness Skills

This task reinforces visual discrimination, problem solving, and eye-hand coordination.

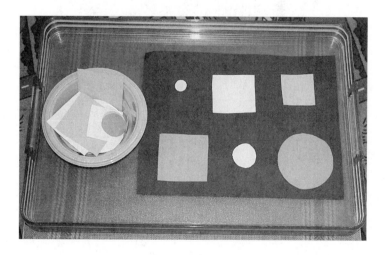

Snap Tray Task

Materials

- ✖ one plastic rectangular tray
- ✖ one snap frame or doll with snap clothing

Setup

Place frame or doll on vertical tray.

Task

Encourage child to use both hands and snap each snap beginning at the top of the frame or doll's outfit and completing to the end.

Outcome

Child successfully attempts to link two sides together snapping.

Readiness Skills

- ■ Child completes a Tray Task by following directions and using top to bottom approach.
- ■ Child uses both hands in coordinated effort that strengthens eye-hand coordination and fine motor skills.

Spatula and Button Tray Task

Materials

- one plastic rectangular tray
- one rubber spatula
- two containers
- buttons

Setup

1. Place tray in horizontal position.
2. Place spatula across the top of the tray.
3. Place containers side by side.
4. Place buttons in the left (first) container.

Task

The child is to pick up the spatula (observe for handedness) and transfer buttons from the left container into the right container.

Outcome

The child's attempt at transferring buttons from one container to another incorporates movements necessary for future reading and writing.

Readiness Skills

This task requires a child to cross the midline and use coordinated movements of both eyes and hands.

Safety Hints

Buttons can be choking hazards. Caution children when using this Tray Task that the buttons remain either on the tray, in the container, or on the transferring instrument.

Spoon and Grain Tray Task

Materials

- one plastic rectangular tray
- two bowls
- one plastic spoon
- one plastic measuring cup of grain (oats, wheat flakes, etc.)

Setup

1. Place tray in horizontal position.
2. Place two bowls on tray side by side.
3. Place spoon across the top of the tray.
4. Place one cup of grain in the first (left) bowl.

Task

- Ask child to pour grain into the first bowl.

- Ask child to transfer grain from the left bowl to the right bowl using a spoon.

Outcome

The child will determine which hand he or she wishes to use to pick up the spoon. The child will attend to the task until completion.

Readiness Skills

This activity encourages the child to use body movements that cross the midline, provide an opportunity to grasp a transfer tool, and emphasize completing a task from left to right.

Tire Tracks Tray Task

Materials

- one plastic rectangular tray
- one truck or car with rubber-tread wheels (small to medium size)
- paper cut to fit inside tray
- paint placed in shallow bowl with blotter

Setup

1. Place tray in a horizontal position.
2. Place paper inside tray.
3. Place shallow bowl with blotter of paint to the left of the tray.
4. Place car or truck inside shallow bowl.

Task

- Child is to transfer truck or car onto the paper and drive it from left to right so that the tire tracks mark the paper.
- The child can make as many left to right tracks as can fit on the paper.

Outcome

By completing this Tray Task, a child will be using the coordinated movements of left-to-right eye and hand tracking.

Readiness Skills

This Tray Task provides a child with the opportunity to grasp a tool that produces marks on paper. This is the same concept as using crayons or pencils and paper.

Tong and Button Tray Task

 ## Materials

 one plastic rectangular tray

one safety tong

buttons

two containers

 ## Setup

1. Place tray in a horizontal position.
2. Place safety tong across top of tray.
3. Place two containers side by side.
4. Place buttons into the first container.

Task

Encourage child to transfer one button at a time using the safety tong.

 ## Outcome

The successful completion of this task causes the child to strengthen his or her grasp of a safety tong while targeting one button at a time for reach and movement.

 ## Readiness Skills

This Tray Task provides observation of a child's handedness, crossing the midline, and coordinating of eyes and hands.

 ## Safety Hints

Remind children that buttons can be a choking hazard. The buttons are to remain on the tray at all times.

Tray Sweeping Tray Task

Materials

- ✖ one plastic rectangular tray
- ✖ one 5-inch circle of solid color contact paper
- ✖ one small handheld whisk broom with scoop
- ✖ one cup of colored rice or small beans
- ✖ one bowl

Setup

1. Adhere contact paper circle to middle of tray.
2. Place whisk broom on left side of tray.
3. Place scoop on left side of tray.
4. Place plastic measuring cup of rice or beans at top of tray.
5. Place bowl to the right on tray.

Task

- ■ The child is to scatter rice or beans on the tray by pouring out measuring cup onto tray.

- ■ Child is to pick up the whisk broom and scoop and place one in each hand.

Outcome

Child is to coordinate movement by sweeping scattered grain into scoop and pouring into bowl until all is swept.

Readiness Skills

This task provides the opportunity for a child to use his or her ability to use both hands in a coordinated way that reflects movements necessary for reading and writing.

Safety Hint

Caution children that the rice or beans used are to remain on the tray.

Tweezer Transfer Tray Task

Materials

- ✖ one plastic rectangular tray
- ✖ one large metal or plastic tweezer
- ✖ two bowls
- ✖ paper confetti or sequins

Setup

1. Place tray in horizontal position.
2. Place large plastic tweezer on left side of tray.
3. Place two bowls side by side next to tweezer.
4. Place paper confetti or sequins in first or left bowl.

Task

Encourage child to pick up the tweezer (observe for handedness) and transfer confetti or sequins one at a time from the left bowl to the right bowl.

Outcome

Child successfully transfers material from the left to the right bowl.

Readiness Skills

By completing this task, a child will be reinforcing grasp control, focusing with eye-hand coordination movements, and strengthening fine motor muscles. This Tray Task is an example of movements used with reading and writing.

Safety Hints

Caution children that tweezers are to be used only on the tray. Use large, metal or plastic, flat-tipped tweezers. Also, the confetti or sequins can be a choking hazard if consumed.

Tying Tray Task

Materials

☒ one plastic rectangular tray

☒ one large shoe with two different colors of shoelaces knotted and laced through a dressing frame or shoe

Setup

1. Place tray in a vertical position.
2. Place shoe vertically on tray.

Task

Child will tie the shoelace and complete a bow.

Outcome

■ Child makes a bow.

■ Child problem-solves, makes decisions, and coordinates movements.

Readiness Skills

The movements used in this task ready the child's body for reading and writing.

Zipper Tray Task

Materials

- ☒ one plastic rectangular tray
- ☒ one dressing frame or a doll with an outfit that has a zipper

Setup

1. Place tray in vertical position.
2. Place doll vertically on tray.

Task

Child is to zip zipper by attaching two ends together and zipping until it is closed.

Outcome

This activity encourages children to problem-solve and refine fine muscles.

Readiness Skills

A child completing this task will strengthen eyes and hands working at the midline.

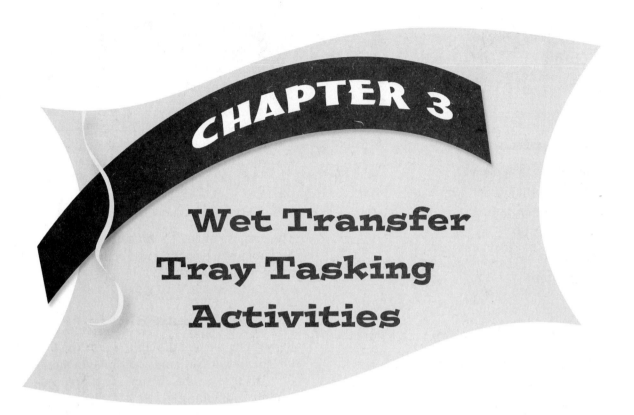

CHAPTER 3

Wet Transfer Tray Tasking Activities

INTRODUCTION

Wet Tray Tasking activities involve the use of water or liquid sources. We introduce water transfer Tray Tasks so that children examine how to control their flow, the level of pouring, and the properties of fluids.

As mentioned, water activities generally calm an active child. The sound liquids make as they pour, the quietness of the activity, and the visual stimulation promote peaceful thinking while completing each task.

AGE RANGE RECOMMENDATIONS

The wet transfer Tray Task activities are written for children from older threes to five years of age. Developmentally, this child should be at an independent learner stage of development and be able to begin and complete a task.

HEALTH AND SAFETY ISSUES

Always change the water or liquid to be used for each child for sanitary and health reasons.

Cleanup supplies should be close by to promote responsibility of cleaning up any spills that may occur. If the learning area is close to a child-sized sink, the child may refill a container and ready it for the next friend when needed.

Cleaning of the containers and transfer instruments can be done by children with soap and water either in the sink or in a large bin. Air-dry them overnight so that you can easily refill the next morning.

DISPLAY IDEAS

Wet transfer Tray Tasks should be displayed on open shelving, preferably on a tiled area of the classroom. Tables and chairs should be nearby. A child may choose to stand or sit with an activity. Label each Tray Task area and tray with words.

Another idea is to take a photograph of each Tray Task and place it on the shelf so that children can see where each tray is to be returned.

STORAGE IDEAS

Wet transfer Tray Task liquids should be emptied each night. Keep containers in your teacher area that can be used to refill water levels, add food coloring, or place other liquids in containers each morning.

Baby Doll Wash Tray Task

Materials

- one plastic rectangular tray
- one bin partially filled with water
- one washable doll
- one washcloth
- hand towel
- soap pump

Setup

1. Place tray in a horizontal position.
2. Place bin partially filled with water on tray.
3. Add several pumps of soap.
4. Place doll in water.
5. Place washcloth to the left of the bin.

Task

- Ask child to wash the doll.
- A child is to use the washcloth as he or she washes the doll.

- When completed, place doll on hand towel and dry.

Outcome

The purpose of doll washing is for the child to use both hands in a coordinated activity that results in a completed task.

Readiness Skills

By washing the doll the child is crossing the midline and using eye-hand coordination motions. Both of these actions mature the skills needed for reading and writing.

Safety Hint

Remember to change the water after each use. You can encourage a child to rinse out the bin with a drying cloth upon completion of the activity. You may also ask each child to refill the bin with water.

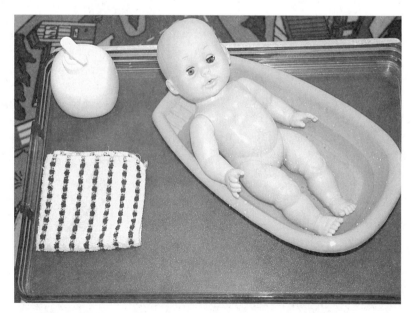

Baster Transfer Tray Task

Materials

- one plastic rectangular tray
- ✖ two plastic bowls (transparent)
- ✖ one baster
- ✖ water mixed with food coloring or liquid color

Setup

1. Place tray in a horizontal position.
2. Place two bowls side by side forming left to right row.
3. Place baster across the top of the tray.
4. Fill first (left) bowl with colored water.

Task

- Child is to transfer colored water from the left to the right bowl using the baster.
- Child may elect to hold the baster with one or two hands to compress the bulb.

Outcome

The goal is to successfully transfer water from the left bowl to the right bowl without spilling any water onto the tray or table.

Readiness Skills

- By completing this task, the child increases his or her ability to coordinate both sides of the body in unison.
- The action repeats the motions necessary for reading and writing.

Safety Hint

Caution the children that a turkey baster and its contents are to be released only into a bowl.

Bubble Beating Tray Task

Materials

- one plastic rectangular tray
- one large bowl
- one handheld rotary eggbeater
- water
- liquid dish detergent

Setup

1. Place tray in a horizontal position.
2. Place large bowl partially filled with bubble water in middle of tray.
3. Place rotary eggbeater across the top of the tray.

Task

- Child will turn the handle on the eggbeater to create bubbles in the bowl.
- By using a handheld eggbeater, the child must coordinate both hands to work in harmony.

Outcome

- By using an eggbeater to beat bubbles in the bowl, the child increases his or her strength in arms, hands, and fingers.
- The child also discovers cause and effect.
- The more the child turns the handle on the beater, the more the child produces bubbles.

Readiness Skills

Strengthens eye-hand coordination, fine muscle development, and completion of a task.

Safety Hint

Have child empty the bubble mixture after completion of the task. Rinse and wipe the bowl and partially refill with water and fresh bubble liquid.

Dish Washing Tray Task

Materials

- ☒ one plastic rectangular tray
- ☒ one large plastic bin or bowl
- ☒ 10 assorted plastic dishes
- ☒ dishwashing detergent
- ☒ dishcloth
- ☒ dishtowel
- ☒ plastic drying rack (optional)

Setup

1. Place tray in a horizontal position.
2. Place large plastic bin or bowl on tray.
3. Fill bin or bowl with water and add dish detergent.
4. Place dishes to the left of the bin or bowl.
5. Placed folded dishcloth to the left of the bin or bowl.
6. Place opened dishtowel to the right of the bowl.

Task

- ■ Child is to wash one dish at a time using the dishcloth.
- ■ After each dish is washed, it is to be placed on the dishtowel.

Outcome

By completing the dish washing Tray Task, the child is discovering cause and effect, problem-solving, and increasing his or her attention to a task until completed.

Readiness Skills

The dishwashing task provides a child with reinforcement of left to right progression using coordinated body movements.

Safety Hints

- ■ Change the dishwashing water after each child's activity is completed.
- ■ You might suggest that the child empty the bin into a child-sized sink, wipe, and refill.

Equal (Same As) Pouring Tray Task

 ## Materials

- one plastic rectangular tray
- two plastic cups
- one plastic 2-cup measuring cup
- water with added liquid color or food coloring

 ## Setup

1. Place tray in a horizontal position.
2. Place two cups filled with colored water on the left side of the tray in a row.
3. Place 2-cup measuring cup on the right side of tray.
4. All cups should be in one row.

 ## Task

- Child is to pour one cup of colored water into the 2-cup measuring cup.
- Then pour the second cup of colored water into the 2-cup cup.

 ## Outcome

- By pouring each cup of water into the 2-cup container, the child will discover that two 1-cup containers equal (or are the same as) one 2-cup container.
- This activity increases math awareness of part to whole and addition.

 ## Readiness Skills

This task strengthens crossing the midline, movement from left to right, and coordinated body motions and increases math skills.

 ## Safety Hint

- Be sure to change the two 1-cup liquids each time the task is selected.
- You might encourage a child to ready the task for a friend at the completion of his or her turn.

 ## Teacher Tip

To extend the learning, use two different primary colors in the water so that when poured, a secondary color will appear.

Eyedropper Tray Task

Materials

✖ one plastic rectangular tray
✖ one large eyedropper
✖ two bowls
✖ water with added color or glitter

Setup

1. Place tray in a horizontal position.
2. Place two bowls side by side in a row.
3. Place eyedropper across the top of the tray.
4. Add colored water to the first or left bowl.

Task

■ Encourage child to pick up the eyedropper (observe for handedness).
■ The task is to transfer the colored water from the left bowl to the right bowl.

Outcome

By transferring water from left to right, the child is increasing his or her awareness of crossing the midline, left to right movement, and completion of a task.

Readiness Skills

This task promotes the pincer grasp, eye-hand coordination, strengthening of fine motor skills, and attention to task.

Safety Hints

■ Cleanse the eyedropper before each child attempts the Tray Task.
■ Suggest to a child that he or she squirt it once or twice under running water so that it does not clog with glitter.

Gelatin Squares Tray Task

Materials

- ✖ one plastic rectangular tray
- ✖ pancake turner
- ✖ two small colorful plates
- ✖ clear-gelled squares (made with clear gelatin mixture)

Setup

1. Place tray in a horizontal position.
2. Place two small plates side by side in a row.
3. Place pancake turner across the top of the tray.
4. Place several gelled squares on the first (left) plate.

Task

Child is to transfer one gelled square at a time from the left plate to the right plate using the pancake turner.

Outcome

- ■ Transferring squares increases the child's ability to focus the body to move in harmony to complete a task.
- ■ This exercise gives the child practice with eye-hand coordination and fine muscle development.

Readiness Skills

This task promotes body movements, left to right progress, and skills necessary for reading and writing readiness.

Safety Hints

- ■ Prepare multiple gelatin squares and keep in a cool place, as you may need to replenish the Tray Task.
- ■ Gelatin squares tend to melt or break apart after repeated usage.

Hand Washing Tray Task

Materials

- one plastic rectangular tray
- one large bowl partially filled with water
- filled liquid hand soap pump
- disposable paper towel

Setup

1. Place tray in a horizontal position.
2. Place bowl filled with water on tray.
3. Place hand pump to the left of the bowl.
4. Place disposable paper towel to the right of the bowl.

Task

- Child is to pump hand soap onto hands and place hands in water.
- Child is to wash hands in rubbing motion.
- Child is to dry hands using paper towel.

Outcome

This task causes child to use both hands in coordinated motions.

Readiness Skills

This task promotes reading and writing readiness by bringing both hands together to work in harmony to complete a washing and drying cycle.

Safety Hints

- Fresh water is to be used each time a child completes this task.
- You might encourage the child to empty, wipe, and refill for a friend.

Ice and Tong Tray Task

 ## Materials

- ✖ one plastic rectangular tray
- ✖ one plastic safety tong
- ✖ one plastic bowl filled with ice cubes
- ✖ one ice cube tray

 ## Setup

1. Place tray in a horizontal position.
2. Place safety tong across the top of the tray.
3. Place plastic bowl filled with ice cubes on the left side of tray.
4. Place ice cube tray, vertically positioned, on the right side of tray.

 ## Task

Child is to use the safety tong and transfer one ice cube at a time from the bowl to the ice cube tray.

Readiness Skills

This task promotes crossing the midline; control of arm, wrist, and finger movement; and coordination of body movement.

Safety Hint

Be sure tong is smooth-edged.

Measuring Liquid Tray Task

Materials

- ✖ one plastic rectangular tray
- ✖ one small plastic pitcher with handle and spout filled with colored water
- ✖ two clear plastic drinking cups, no handles
- ✖ two colored rubber bands

Setup

1. Place tray in horizontal position.
2. Place rubber band around both cups at any point on each cup.
3. Place small pitcher on the left side of the tray.
4. Place two plastic drinking cups side by side next to the pitcher.

Task

The child is to pour from the pitcher into the cups up to the rubber band.

Outcome

By pouring colored water from the pitcher into each cup, the child must make a decision as to how far to pour to each marked level.

Readiness Skills

This task requires the child to grasp the handle and coordinate movements with eye-hand coordination with left to right progression.

Mirror Washing Tray Task

 ## Materials

- ✖ one plastic rectangular tray
- ✖ one small safety mirror in a plastic frame
- ✖ one small squirt bottle filled with soapy water
- ✖ one paper towel

 ## Setup

1. Place tray in a horizontal position.
2. Place small safety mirror in middle of tray.
3. Place squirt bottle on left of mirror.
4. Place paper towel on right of mirror.

 ## Task

The child will squirt the mirror then wipe with paper towel.

Outcome

This task requires child to cross the midline and use both hands to coordinate body movement.

Readiness Skills

Child is using readiness skills that promote reading and writing.

Safety Hint

Be sure mirror has safe edge around it, such as plastic.

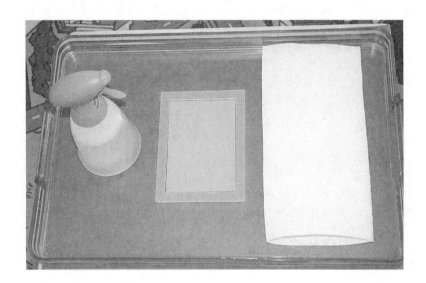

Pipette Tray Task

 ## Materials

- ✖ one plastic rectangular tray
- ✖ one pipette or slender eyedropper
- ✖ one clear gelatin mold
- ✖ plate
- ✖ cup with colored water

 ## Setup

1. Place tray in horizontal position.
2. Place prepared gelatin mold on plate in middle of tray.
3. Place pipette on the left side of mold.
4. Place cup filled with colored water between pipette and plate.

 ## Task

- ■ Child is to pick up the pipette, fill with colored water from cup, and squeeze water solution by inserting pipette into mold.
- ■ To vary this activity, you may offer more than one color of water.

 ## Outcome

Child crosses midline, coordinates eye-hand motions, and discovers the properties of seeing color disperse throughout the gelatin mold.

 ## Readiness Skills

Pincer control and fine muscle development are strengthened, which are needed for writing.

Pouring and Measuring Tray Task

Materials

 one plastic rectangular tray

 one clear plastic cup

 one 2-cup plastic measuring cup

 colored water

Setup

1. Place tray in horizontal position.
2. Place cup filled with colored water on left side of tray.
3. Place measuring cup on right side of tray.

Task

Child is to transfer water from cup to 1-cup line on measuring cup.

Outcome

Child demonstrates ability to stop pouring at specific level.

Readiness Skills

Reaching for cup, holding cup with one hand, and steadily pouring to specific level all prepare child for reading and writing by strengthening grasp control with hands.

Teacher Tip

Teacher can mark 1-cup level with rubber band or colored tape.

Sand and Water Tray Task

Materials

- [x] one plastic rectangular tray
- [x] one large bowl
- [x] one cup of sand
- [x] one cup of water
- [x] one serving spoon

Setup

1. Place tray in a horizontal position.
2. Place two small containers on left side of tray.
3. Place large bowl on right side of tray.
4. Place serving spoon across the top of tray.

Task

- Child will pour sand into bowl and pour water into bowl.
- Using the spoon, child will slowly mix until sand and water are mixed.

Outcome

Child's ability to mix thoroughly will demonstrate hand control and coordination.

Readiness Skills

Mixing causes child to continuously cross the midline, which is needed in preparation for reading and writing.

Safety Hints

- Refill container of sand and container of water each time or have child do this at a preparation table or near a sink area.
- Keep extra sand in small, easily poured container.

Seashell Wash Tray Task

Materials

- one plastic rectangular tray
- one large conch shell
- one nailbrush or vegetable brush with handle
- liquid soap and water
- small bowl

Setup

1. Place tray in a horizontal position.
2. Place conch shell on tray.
3. Place nailbrush or vegetable brush at top of tray.
4. Place liquid soap and water in small bowl.

Task

- Child dips brush into soapy water and brushes the conch shell.
- Child turns shell around to enter all areas of shell.

Readiness Skills

- Holding the brush increases child's ability to grasp and control movement.
- Moving brush in all areas requires crossing the midline and using eye-hand coordination.
- All of these actions are necessary for reading and writing.

Safety Hint

Be sure to have child change water after completing the task.

Sink and Float Tray Task

 ## Materials

- one plastic rectangular tray
- small basket
- small objects that sink and float
- clear bowl filled with water
- one solid color vinyl placemat fitted to length of tray or a tray with a column design

 ## Setup

1. Place tray in a vertical or horizontal position (depends on the design).
2. Place small basket filled with objects to the top of the tray.
3. Place bowl of water below small basket and tray.
4. Draw line lengthwise down middle of placemat; label one side "sink," the other side "float."

Task

- Child is to transfer one small object at a time into the water, then determine whether it sinks or floats.
- Place object in correct column on tray until completed.

 ## Outcome

Child completes a fun task by scientifically making a decision.

 ## Readiness Skills

Child crosses midline and moves in a left to right direction.

 ## Safety Hint

Have child change water after completion of the task.

 ## Teacher Tip

Discuss and show the words sink and float. Add graphics such as a waterline with an object drawn on the line for "float" and a waterline with an object drawn below the line for "sink."

Small Cup with No Handles Tray Task

Materials

- ✘ one plastic rectangular tray
- ✘ one small plastic cup without handles
- ✘ one container
- ✘ colored water

Setup

1. Place tray in horizontal position.
2. Place cup filled with colored water on left side of tray.
3. Place container on right side of tray.

Task

Child is to pour water from cup into container.

Outcome

Child must determine how to hold cup because it has no handles.

Readiness Skills

Child coordinates movement of both hands and arms and crosses the midline.

Small Pitcher with Handle Tray Task

 ## Materials

- one plastic rectangular tray
- one small plastic pitcher with a handle and a spout
- colored water
- small container

 ## Setup

1. Place tray in horizontal position.
2. Place small plastic pitcher filled with colored water on left side of tray.
3. Place small container on right side of tray.

 ## Task

Child is to pour water from pitcher into container.

Outcome

If child is successful, he or she will pour water without spilling.

 ## Readiness Skills

Child is crossing the midline and using both arms and hands in coordinated movement and refining eye-hand control.

Sponge Squeeze Tray Task

 ## Materials

 one plastic rectangular tray

one large sponge

one large bowl partially filled with water

one empty large bowl

Setup

1. Place tray in horizontal position.
2. Place bowls side by side, with filled bowl on the left.
3. Place sponge at the top of the tray.

Task

 Child is to place sponge into first bowl and soak up water into sponge.

Child is to transfer water from first bowl into second bowl by squeezing sponge full of water into second bowl.

Continue action until all water is transferred.

Readiness Skills

 This task causes child to use both hands in coordinated way.

Child increases use of grasping and squeezing, both needed to hold a pencil.

Child moves from left to right, actions needed for reading and writing.

Safety Hint

Change out water each time after a child completes the task.

Spooning Liquid Tray Task

Materials

- one plastic rectangular tray
- two clear plastic bowls
- one large serving spoon
- water mixed with glitter and/or sequins to add visual effect

Setup

1. Place tray in horizontal position.
2. Place two bowls side by side.
3. Place spoon across top of tray.
4. Fill first bowl (left) with liquid mixture.

Task

Child will pick up spoon (observe for handedness) and transfer water from left to right bowl.

Outcome

Child will continue task until all water is transferred.

Readiness Skills

Picking up the spoon from the top of the tray and moving in a left to right direction are both motions that prepare the child for reading and writing.

Safety Hint

Glitter or sequins can be hazardous if not used properly.

Syringe Tray Task

 Materials

- ✖ one plastic rectangular tray
- ✖ one syringe
- ✖ two bowls
- ✖ water with food coloring

 Setup

1. Place tray in a horizontal position.
2. Place syringe at top of tray.
3. Place two bowls side by side.
4. Place colored water into first bowl.

 Task

Child is to transfer water from the left to the right bowl, using a syringe.

Outcome

Upon completion, the water should be transferred from left to right bowl with minimal (or no) spilling.

Readiness Skills

Transferring requires the body to move in a coordinated motion from left to right.

Table Washing Tray Task

 ## Materials

- one plastic rectangular tray
- several disposable paper towels
- one small sponge
- small bowl
- water
- liquid soap

Setup

1. Place tray in vertical position.
2. Place small bowl filled with water and soap on tray.
3. Place small sponge at top of bowl.
4. Place paper towels to right of bowl.

 ## Task

- Child is to dip small sponge into soapy water and begin to make circular motions on table for washing.
- Child completes washing cycle.
- Child uses paper towels to dry table.

 ## Outcome

By washing and drying the table, the child completes a cleaning cycle.

 ## Readiness Skills

This task involves the child in motions that coordinate body movements, refine eye-hand coordination, and move in circular pattern similar to pencil writing.

Water Color Mixing Tray Task

 Materials

- ✖ one plastic rectangular tray
- ✖ three see-through plastic glasses
- ✖ food coloring
- ✖ water

Setup

1. Place tray in horizontal position.
2. Place three glasses in one row on tray.
3. Fill first two glasses with a primary food color and water in each.

Task

Child is to slowly pour a small amount of each primary color into empty glass and mix, and then watch results.

Outcome

Child discovers that a new color has been formed.

Readiness Skills

By pouring water and mixing colors, a child strengthens visual discrimination as well as crosses the midline and coordinates body movements.

Safety Hint

Glasses should be cleaned and refilled with appropriate color water each time.

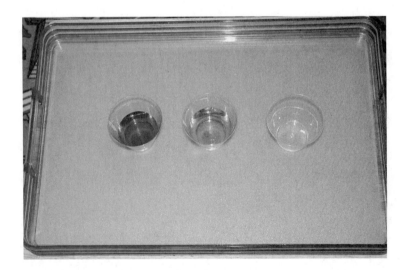

Water Pouring Tray Task

 ## Materials

 one plastic rectangular tray

one watering can with spout and handle filled with water

one small, nonpoisonous plant

 ## Setup

1. Place tray in horizontal position.
2. Place plant on right side of tray.
3. Place small watering can on left side of tray.

Task

Child will pick up watering can and water plant.

 ## Outcome

Plant will receive water without child spilling water on table or floor.

 ## Readiness Skills

- Child determines which hand or uses both hands to hold watering can.
- Child crosses midline and promotes left to right movements.

 ## Safety Hint

Have more than one plant so that children do not overwater the same plant each time.

Wire Whisk Tray Task

Materials

 one plastic rectangular tray

 one wire whisk

 one large bowl

 one small container of cornmeal

 water

Setup

1. Place tray in horizontal position.
2. Place large bowl in middle of tray.
3. Place wire whisk across top of tray.
4. Place cornmeal and water in bowl.

Task

Child is to use wire whisk and stir the cornmeal-and-water mixture.

Outcome

Mixture will be combined.

Readiness Skills

This task promotes a circular motion that a child will use when writing.

Safety Hint

Change out water and cornmeal each time.

CHAPTER 4

Arranging Your Small Manipulatives and Math Center

INTRODUCTION

Your Small Manipulatives and/or Math Learning Center probably contain materials that children use for sorting, connecting, counting, matching, sequencing, and classifying. All these skills can be captured with Tray Tasking by organizing materials in easy-to-use activities.

This is a very important area of your learning environment. This area provides opportunities for your children to investigate the properties of materials while engaging their fingers and hands in a coordinated effort to achieve a successful completion of an activity. Every item in this area is a reading and writing readiness task.

Take a moment and look at your small manipulative learning center. Use the following guidelines:

1. Follow the three A's:
   - All materials should be *accessible*.
   - All materials should be *available*.
   - All materials should be *attractive*.

2. Separate the multipiece activities into several tasks.

3. The use of color-coordinated baskets and trays helps a child learn that there is a place for everything and everything has a place.

4. Label all learning activities with pictures and words.

5. Rearrange your area with new or extended activities when you notice children's interests change, usually every six weeks.

Incorporate the following ideas when redesigning your area:

- Assemble one task per tray.
- How you display materials sets the tone for learning.
- Teacher-made activities are cost-effective.
- Increase longevity of current materials by dividing sets into several tasks.
- When using folder games, display using vertically positioned trays.

The following Tray Tasks are a few examples of how you can expand your learning options for young children. Each task shows you ways you can set up more than one of each of these tasks for more child choices.

Addition Tray Task

 ### Materials

 one plastic rectangular tray

a set of large domino tiles or cards (teacher-made or store-bought)

small basket

Setup

1. Place tray in a horizontal position.

2. Select two low-numbered domino tiles or cards and place side by side on the tray.

3. Place a + sign between them and an = sign after them.

4. Place a small basket of domino tiles or cards on the left of the tray.

 ### Task

■ Child is to continuously count all the dots on both cards

■ Child is to look at the possible answers in the small basket and select a card that displays the total of the dots from both tiles or cards.

 ### Outcome

This task provides a child with an opportunity to construct meaning and problem-solve by using domino cards for an addition equation.

 ### Readiness Skills

Child strengthens visual acuity and eye tracking by moving from left to right while counting the cards.

Block Tray Task

Materials

- one plastic rectangular tray
- one container
- 20 blocks that connect

Setup

1. Place tray in horizontal position.
2. Place blocks in container.
3. Place container on left of tray.

Task

Ask child to construct a structure using blocks in container.

Outcome

Child builds a creative structure while reinforcing eye-hand coordination, arm and wrist strengthening, and centering at the midline.

Readiness Skills

Child is refining eye tracking and spatial relationships.

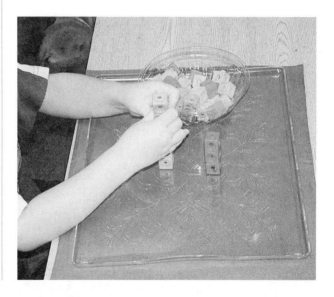

Geoboard Tray Task

Materials

- one plastic rectangular tray
- one geoboard
- one small container
- six colored rubber bands

Setup

1. Place tray in horizontal position.
2. Place geoboard in middle of tray.
3. Place small container to left of geoboard.
4. Place rubber bands inside container.

Task

Child will select one band at a time to stretch on the board of nails to make a design.

Outcome

Teacher can make instruction cards showing six colors of bands stretched around different nails for child to follow, or child can randomly make a design.

Readiness Skills

This task encourages child to use fine motor skills when stretching bands, eye-hand coordination, and focusing body to center of midline.

Safety Hints

- Talk with your children about the safety hazards of rubber bands.
- The rubber bands are to remain on the tray or board only.

Lacing Cards Tray Task

Materials

 one plastic rectangular tray

 one lacing card

 one lace

Setup

1. Place tray in horizontal position.
2. Place lacing card on tray.
3. Place lace across the top of tray.

Task

- Ask child to hold card in one hand and place a lace in the other and weave in and out of the card.

- Teacher should observe for handedness and ability for each hand to perform a different task at the same time.

Outcome

Child will complete lacing the card.

Readiness Skills

Child will coordinate body motions while maintaining balance using both hands to accomplish different skill levels.

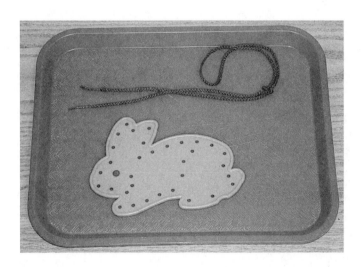

Pegboard Tray Task

 ## Materials

✖ one plastic rectangular tray

✖ one pegboard

✖ one small container

✖ predetermined color and number of pegs

✖ pegboard paper template strip

 ## Setup

1. Place tray in horizontal position.

2. Place pegboard on tray.

3. Place teacher-made template strip down first column of holes. Make sure that there is a different color per row.

4. Place pegs in small container and place on left side of pegboard.

 ## Task

Ask child to place pegs in row in pegboard according to color code, starting at the top of the pegboard.

 ## Outcome

Child uses problem-solving to determine which pegs go in which row.

 ## Readiness Skills

Child works top to bottom and left to right to complete this task.

Pop Beads Tray Task

 ## Materials

 one plastic rectangular tray

 10 plastic pop beads

 one bowl

Setup

1. Place tray in horizontal position.
2. Place bowl in middle of tray.
3. Place beads inside bowl.

 ## Task

Ask child to snap beads together into a necklace.

 ## Outcome

Child will use both hands to complete the task.

 ## Readiness Skills

- This task focuses child's eyes and hands toward the middle of the midline.
- It causes the hands to work together to achieve success.

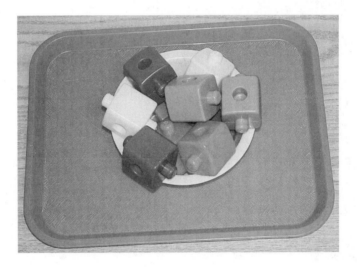

Puzzle Tray Task

 ## Materials

 one plastic rectangular tray
wooden puzzle in frame

 ## Setup

1. Place tray in either horizontal or vertical position according to puzzle.

2. Place all puzzle pieces to left of tray.

Task

Ask child to complete wooden puzzle by selecting

one piece at a time from the left and moving it to the right and onto the puzzle frame.

 ## Outcome

Child will visualize completed puzzle while determining which piece to select next.

 ## Readiness Skills

Child is using left to right directions and crossing the midline as he or she completes the puzzle.

Used by permission of Small World Toys

Repeating Color (or Shape) Bead Pattern Tray Task

Materials

- ☒ one plastic rectangular tray
- ☒ preselected beads, two colors (or shapes), six of each color (or shape)
- ☒ one bead pattern card only showing six beads in alternating colors (or shapes)
- ☒ one lacing string
- ☒ small basket

Setup

1. Place tray in a horizontal position.
2. Place small basket containing six beads on left of tray.
3. Place string across top of tray.
4. Secure bead pattern card across bottom portion of tray.

Task

- Child is to string beads by matching pattern.
- Ask child to decide what comes next to complete the pattern so that there are six beads on the string.

Outcome

Child will successfully complete task when making a decision about what bead color (or shape) comes next.

Readiness Skills

Problem-solving tasks are important. They provide a child with an opportunity to make a decision according to the purpose of the task.

Teacher Tips

- To make the repeating bead pattern card, use sentence strip paper and draw six beads according to the pattern you want the child to repeat. The pattern could be red bead, green bead, red bead, and so on; or sphere, cube, sphere, and so on.
- The child will have to problem-solve and select the right color (or shape) of bead to match the pattern card when stringing.

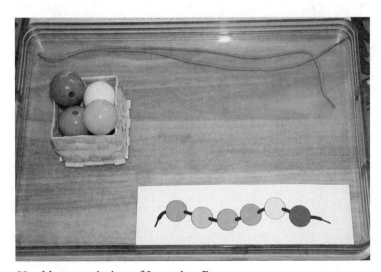

Used by permission of Learning Resources

Small Blocks Stacking Tray Task

 ## Materials

- ✖ one plastic rectangular tray
- ✖ one bowl
- ✖ an assortment of small blocks in four colors using five of each color

 ## Setup

1. Place tray in horizontal position.
2. Place bowl on left side of tray.
3. Place small blocks in bowl.

 ## Task

Ask child to build towers of blocks with each tower being one color.

 ## Outcome

Child will successfully select same color blocks per tower and stack to make four five-block towers.

Readiness Skills

- This task provides child with the opportunity to refine small muscle control, use arm and wrist movements, and enhance eye-hand coordination.
- Stacking also strengthens the centering of the midline.

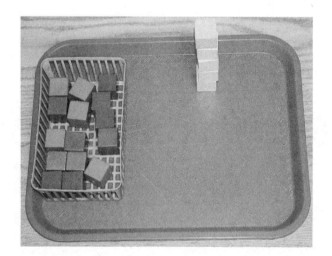

Take Away Tray Task

Materials

✖ one plastic rectangular tray

✖ one small plastic plate

✖ five plastic animals

✖ small bowl

✖ teacher-made cards showing numerals 1–5

Setup

1. Place tray in a horizontal position.

2. Place plastic plate on the left side of the tray.

3. Place five plastic animals on plate.

4. Place cards in small basket on the right side of the tray.

Task

■ Ask child to count how many animals are on the plate.

■ Tell child to take away two of them.

■ Ask child to find a card that depicts how many animals are now on the plate and place it below the plate.

Outcome

Child uses problem-solving and decision-making skills in deciding how many animals are left when some are taken away.

Readiness Skills

Math skills are refined when opportunities for counting and sorting occur.

Teacher Tip

For children who are not ready to identify numerals, use quantity cards with circles or other shapes instead.

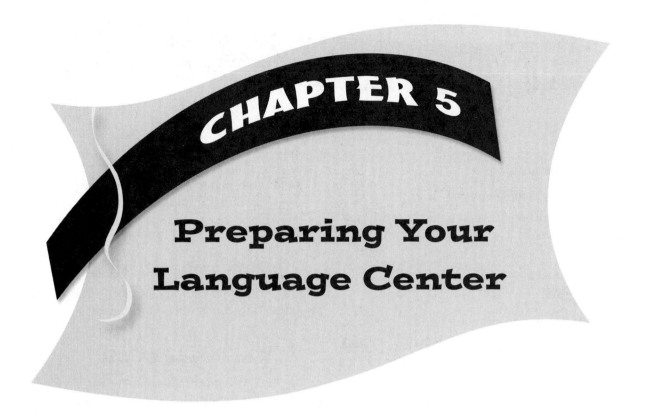

CHAPTER 5

Preparing Your Language Center

The Language Learning Center area of your classroom contains reading and writing readiness opportunities. Tray Tasking can help define the intended learning outcomes and help identify and observe your children's skills and abilities.

The following are examples of ways you can reorganize your area to reflect a Tray Tasking display. The following guidelines are similar to what was discussed in the previous chapter:

1. Follow the three A's:

   - All materials should be *accessible.*

   - All materials should be *available.*

   - All materials should be *attractive.*

2. Separate language materials into singular activities.

3. The use of color-coordinated baskets and trays help a child learn that there is a place for everything and everything has a place.

4. Label all learning activities with pictures and words.

5. Rearrange your area with new or extended

activities when you notice children's interests change, usually every six weeks.

Incorporate the following ideas when redesigning your area:

- Assemble one task per tray.

- How you display materials sets the tone for learning.

- Teacher-made activities are cost-effective.

- Increase longevity of current materials by dividing sets into several tasks.

- When using folder games, display using vertically positioned trays.

Several writing Tray Tasks are included in this section to suggest several ways to incorporate prewriting activities into learning centers, either in language, art, or as a separate writing area. Take the lead and continue to create Tray Tasks utilizing the materials you have in the classroom.

Blanket Tray Task

Materials

- ✖ one plastic rectangular tray
- ✖ one sheet of construction paper cut to fit tray
- ✖ crayons

Setup

1. Place tray in horizontal position.
2. Fold construction paper so that there are four squares resembling a folded blanket when opened.
3. Place paper on tray.
4. Place crayons to left of tray.

Task

Teacher is to call out a color, shape, and a location. For example: "Draw one blue circle in the top left corner of the blanket." "Draw four red triangles in the bottom right corner of the blanket." "Draw two green diamonds in the top right corner." "Draw three black squares in the bottom left corner."

Outcome

Child will listen to direction and draw the answer in the proper location on the blanket.

Readiness Skills

- ■ This activity combines auditory discrimination and visual discrimination as the child decides what color to choose, what shape to draw, how many to draw, and where to place the shape on the blanket.
- ■ The directions reinforce top to bottom and left to right directionalities.

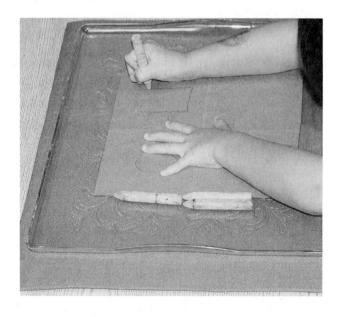

Lazy Eight Tray Task

 Materials

✖ one plastic rectangular tray
✖ dried glue in the shape of a horizontal lazy eight figure on paper

 Setup

1. Place tray in horizontal position.
2. Place paper in horizontal position on the tray.

 Task

Child uses fingers to press and continually trace over the lazy eight starting from the left side, up, across, down, across, and back.

 Outcome

Child uses the crossing of the midline motion to reinforce the body's ability to move in harmony with eyes and hands following a repeated movement.

 Readiness Skills

This activity promotes the basic body movement for left to right and top to bottom movements needed for reading and writing.

 Variation

■ Try cutting lazy eight figure from sandpaper or cardboard and place on a clipboard.
■ Cut lazy eight figure out of tagboard and lay tagboard outline on tray on top of paper and place colored pencils on left side of tray for child to continually trace the figure eight pattern.

Letter Forming Tray Task

Materials

- one plastic rectangular tray
- two vinyl or laminated letter outlines
- play dough or yarn

Setup

1. Place tray in horizontal position.
2. Select single vinyl letter or letters that are theme-related.
3. Place play dough or yarn on left side of tray.

Task

Encourage child to form and place play dough or lay yarn on the letter outlines.

Outcome

This task allows a child to concentrate on one or two letter formations while using hands to outline lines and shapes of letters.

Readiness Skills

Child is discovering the differences and similarities of letter shapes using visual discrimination and tactile stimulation.

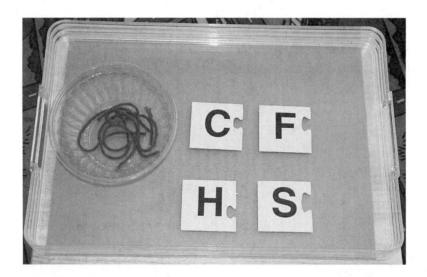

Name Tray Task

Materials

- ✗ one plastic rectangular tray
- ✗ sentence strips with children's first names on them
- ✗ paper cut to fit over name strip
- ✗ individually cut letters for each child in individual envelopes with name printed on front

Setup

1. Place tray in horizontal position.
2. Select a child's sentence strip name and place across middle of tray.
3. Place cut paper to the left of tray.
4. Place envelope with child's name on it across top of tray.

Task

- ■ Ask child to identify his or her name on tray.
- ■ Ask child to cover name with cut paper.
- ■ Ask child to open envelope of his or her name letters.
- ■ Child is to place letters in correct sequence to spell his or her name.
- ■ Child uncovers paper and reveals sentence strip name to see match.

Outcome

This task helps a child see letter to name connection and reinforces left to right directionality.

Readiness Skills

By completing this task, a child is connecting oral and written language.

Personalized Tray Task

 ## Materials

- one plastic rectangular tray
- sentence strip paper
- black marker (write each child's name on a sentence strip twice)
- plain paper cut to cover sentence strip name
- basket

 ## Setup

1. Place tray in horizontal position.
2. Write and display several children's first names, each on a sentence strip.
3. Cut up second set of sentence strips and put all of the children's name letters in basket.

 ## Task

- Child is to select his or her name from the group and place it across the top of the tray.
- Child is to place the rest of the names to the left of the tray.
- Child selects letters from basket to form his or her name and places letters in a row beneath the covered sentence strip.

 ## Outcome

Child reinforces sequencing of letters to form a word by organizing letters in his or her first name.

Readiness Skills

- The child integrates left to right progression into this task.
- Child can check his or her work by lifting up the paper that is covering name to verify that letters are placed in correct order.

Rhyming Tray Task

 ## Materials

- ✖ one plastic rectangular tray
- ✖ three picture cards
- ✖ three more picture cards that rhyme with the first three picture cards
- ✖ small basket

 ## Setup

1. Place tray in vertical position.
2. Tape three pictures to the tray vertically on left side of tray.
3. Place basket with rhyming words at top of tray.

 ## Task

- ■ Ask child to name the three pictures on the tray.
- ■ Child is to select a picture from the basket and place it next to the picture with which it rhymes.

 ## Outcome

- ■ Child is to complete all three picture matches.
- ■ Child says names of rhyming pairs out loud.

 ## Readiness Skills

Practice with picture to sound relationships.

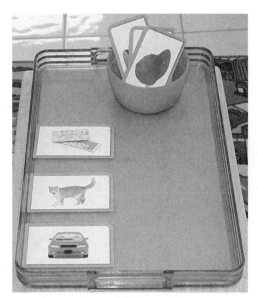

Rhyming *Pocket Flash Cards used by permission of TREND enterprises, Inc., St. Paul, Minnesota,* www.trendenter prises.com.

Straight Line Tracing Tray Task

Materials

✖ one plastic rectangular tray
✖ one sheet of paper with two-inch straight lines drawn from left to right

Setup

1. Place tray in horizontal position.
2. Select from the following variety of hands-on tools for line tracing:
   - colored chalk
   - fingerpaint
   - colored pencils
   - markers
   - crayons

Task

- Place lined paper on tray.
- Place the selected tools on the left side of the tray.
- Child is to trace over the lines with various colors from left to right.

Outcome

Child will reinforce left to right directions and handedness by tracing the straight lines with various colored tools.

Readiness Skills

This activity resembles a writing activity as child moves tool from left to right.

Swirled Line Tracing Tray Task

 ## Materials

- one plastic rectangular tray
- one sheet of paper with continual two-inch swirled lines extending from left to right
- colored pencils
- basket (if desired)

 ## Setup

1. Place tray in horizontal position.
2. Place paper on tray.
3. Place basket to the left of tray.
4. Place colored pencils in basket.

 ## Task

Child will select a pencil and continually trace swirled lines on the paper.

 ## Outcome

Child is utilizing his ability to follow continual lines.

Readiness Skills

Reinforcement of eye tracking as well as eye-hand coordination and grasp control.

Two-Handed Drawing Tray Task

 ## Materials

- one plastic rectangular tray
- paper cut to fit tray
- crayons
- basket

 ## Setup

1. Place tray in horizontal position.
2. Place one sheet of paper on tray.
3. Place crayons in basket on left of tray.

 ## Task

- Child selects one crayon per hand.

- Child begins at the middle of the paper and draws continuous lines toward the outer edges of tray.
- The line drawings are to be identical to each other.

 ## Outcome

This activity reinforces the handedness of the child. It provides an opportunity to use opposing movements.

 ## Readiness Skills

This activity promotes eye-hand control of movement and moving from the inward to the outward stretch of the body.

Word Forming Tray Task

Materials

- ✘ one plastic rectangular tray
- ✘ individual letters for simple three-letter words (cat, mat, hat, etc.)
- ✘ several small pictures (with no words) of word choices
- ✘ small basket

Setup

1. Place tray in horizontal position.
2. Laminate or adhere two ending letters in middle and right side of tray.
3. Place small basket at top of tray.
4. Place remaining letters and small pictures in basket.

Task

- Ask child to tell you what letters are on the tray.
- Sound out the letters in the basket.
- Child selects one letter and places it on left side of the other two letters.
- Ask child to sound out the word from left to right.
- Child selects the one picture that depicts the word and places it to the left of the word.

Outcome

Child has opportunity to connect written and spoken words.

Readiness Skills

Child forms simple three-letter words and reinforces word to picture relationship, which is reading readiness practice.

Teacher Tips

- Write the word on the back of each picture card that tells what the picture is so that Tray Task can be self-checking.
- Child can turn card over and compare to three letters on tray. Are they the same?

CHAPTER 6

Accommodating Your Science Center

INTRODUCTION

One way to arrange your Science Learning Center is through the use of Tray Tasks. The following guidelines are similar to what was discussed in the previous chapter:

1. Follow the three A's:
   - All materials should be *accessible*.
   - All materials should be *available*.
   - All materials should be *attractive*.

2. Separate science materials into singular activities.

3. The use of color-coordinated baskets and trays help a child learn that there is a place for everything and everything has a place.

4. Label all learning activities with pictures and words.

5. Rearrange your area with new or extended activities when you notice children's interests change, usually every six weeks.

Incorporate the following ideas when redesigning your area:

- Assemble one task per tray.
- How you display materials sets the tone for learning.
- Teacher-made activities are cost-effective.
- Increase longevity of current materials by dividing sets into several tasks.
- When using folder games, display using vertically positioned trays.

Use a Science Tray Task as a technique to begin a new topic of discussion, a new theme, or a new science focus. By presenting a new concept or experiment using a tray, you can display the tools necessary for children to explore the properties of life science, collections, weather, solar systems, and other topics of interest.

Applesauce Tray Task

 ## Materials

- one plastic rectangular tray
- three diced wedges of apples (drop or two of lemon juice added)
- handheld potato masher
- cinnamon sugar in shaker
- paper cup
- plastic spoon

 ## Setup

1. Place tray in horizontal position.
2. Place one mixing bowl filled with diced wedges of apples in middle of tray.
3. Place handheld potato masher across top of tray.
4. Place shaker, cup, and spoon to right of bowl.

 ## Task

- Ask child to mash apples with handheld potato masher.
- Spoon mixture into paper cup.
- Add a dash of cinnamon sugar.
- Enjoy as a snack with a cracker or bread.

 ## Outcome

Child is discovering the properties of apples and how apples change when acted upon.

 ## Readiness Skills

Child is using midline, eye-hand coordination, and focus while strengthening arm and hand muscles needed for future writing.

 ## Safety Hint

Dice fresh apple wedges for each Tray Task activity.

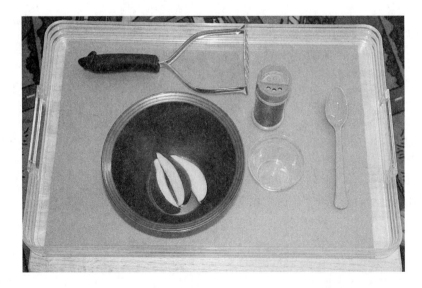

Arrow Tray Task

 ## Materials

- ✖ one plastic rectangular tray
- ✖ two index cards, showing an arrow on both cards
- ✖ six nature pictures of objects that either fly in the sky or swim in the ocean mounted on index cards such as
  —eagle/sea turtle
  —owl/stingray
  —robin/fish
- ✖ bowl for pictures

Setup

1. Place tray in vertical position.
2. Place one arrow pointing up and place arrow pointing down next to it to create two columns.
3. Place bowl of pictures one left corner of tray.

 ## Task

Encourage child to sort pictures and select which ones go in the "fly in the sky" column and which ones go in the "swim in the ocean" column.

 ## Outcome

Child will use problem-solving skills to sort and classify.

 ## Readiness Skills

Child is crossing midline while sorting and moving in top to bottom and left to right directions on the tray.

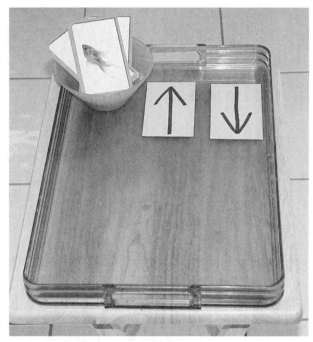

Rhyming *Pocket Flash Cards used by permission of TREND enterprises, Inc., St. Paul, Minnesota, www.trendenterprises.com.*

Go Together Tray Task

 Materials

- ✖ one plastic rectangular tray
- ✖ pictures of three sets of items that go together such as
    —shoes/socks
    —toothbrush/toothpaste
    —brush/comb
- ✖ three strings of yarn
- ✖ poster board cut to fit tray
- ✖ six brass fasteners

 Setup

1. Place tray in vertical position.
2. Cut poster board to fit vertical tray.
3. Section poster board into two columns of three spaces each.
4. Glue one column of pictures, one below the other showing one of a go-together mate.
5. Attach a brass fastener to the left of each picture.
6. Glue second column of pictures out of order from their mates.
7. Create another column of brass fasteners to the right of the pictures.
8. Attach one string of yarn to each of the first brass fasteners.

 Task

- ■ Ask child to look at the pictures.

- ■ When child thinks he or she has found a mate, the child is to take a yarn string and twist it across and around the mate's brass fastener.

 Outcome

Child will use problem-solving skills and think about what goes together in order to solve this Tray Task.

 Readiness Skills

- ■ Child will use small finger muscles to coordinate the yarn around the brass fasteners.
- ■ The child is crossing midline to accomplish this Tray Task.
- ■ The child is using eye-hand coordination and left to right progression skills.

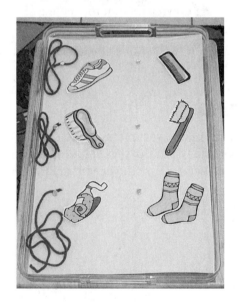

Graduated Color Chips Tray Task

 ## Materials

- one plastic rectangular tray
- one plastic bowl
- paint chip cards from hardware store of graduated shades and tints of three or four colors

 ## Setup

1. Place tray in horizontal position.
2. Place bowl containing paint chip cards at top left corner of tray.

Task

Child is to arrange rows of same color chip cards from dark to light or light to dark.

 ## Outcome

The child will use problem-solving and visual discrimination skills to sort paint chip cards by color and by shades and tints placing rows in a left to right progression.

 ## Readiness Skills

By sorting paint chip cards in this way, the child is applying concentration skills, eye-hand coordination, and eye tracking as well as crossing the midline multiple times to assemble rows of chips.

Heavy to Light Weight Tray Task

 ## Materials

- one plastic rectangular tray
- collection of rocks and small pebbles
- two bowls
- tong

 ## Setup

1. Place tray in horizontal position.
2. Place bowl containing rocks and pebbles on left of tray.
3. Place empty bowl to right of first bowl.
4. Place tong across top of tray.

 ## Task

Ask child to dip tong into bowl and transfer collection from heavy to light or from light to heavy.

 ## Outcome

Child will use decision-making and problem-solving skills while selecting pebbles and rocks in sequence order.

 ## Readiness Skills

Child will use small muscles in arms, hands, and fingers to coordinate the movement of left to right progression of rock and pebble collection.

 ## Safety Hint

Small pebbles can be a choking or inhaling hazard. Remind children that all rocks and pebbles remain on the tray.

 ## Teacher Tip

A variation to this Tray Task is to use only the bowl filled with pebbles and rocks and encourage a child to select only the lightweight pebbles with fingers and place in a row from left to right across tray. Or ask child to make a pattern such as light, light, heavy, light, light, heavy, and so on.

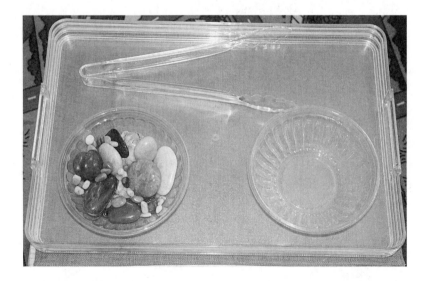

Magnet Attraction Tray Task

 ## Materials

 one plastic rectangular tray

 metal paper clips

 plastic coated paper clips in various colors

 magnet wand

 two bowls

 ## Setup

1. Place tray in horizontal position.

2. Place two small bowls side by side on tray.

3. Place both plastic and metal clips in left bowl.

4. Place magnet wand across top of tray.

Task

Ask child to transfer paper clips from the left to the right bowl.

 ## Outcome

■ Which clips were attracted to the magnet? Why?

■ Child is exploring the properties of magnetism.

 ## Readiness Skills

The activity provides the opportunity of learning about magnets and their properties. The child will see what is and is not attracted to the magnet with the metal and plastic clip choices.

Mixture Making Tray Task

 ## Materials

 one plastic rectangular tray

½ cup of liquid starch

½ cup of white glue

 ## Setup

1. Place tray in horizontal position.
2. Place two cups one above the other on left side of tray.

 ## Task

■ Child is to pour both cups directly onto tray.

■ Child is to use hands to merge two mixtures together to create a new substance.

 ## Outcome

■ Child creates a new substance from two in-gredients.

■ Child uses discovery and exploration methods to create new consistency to the substance.

 ## Readiness Skills

This Tray Task promotes two-handed coordination, using hands in harmony, and visual discrimination.

 ## Safety Hint

When mixed, this mixture turns into a taffy-type texture. It is not for eating or placing anywhere else but on the tray.

Teacher Tips

■ Encourage child to mold and create designs with the mixture then roll into a ball and place in a bag for storage.

■ If you wish to add color, mix one drop of food coloring into the glue cup before child creates a new substance.

■ Ask child to wash and wipe the tray dry so that the next friend can begin.

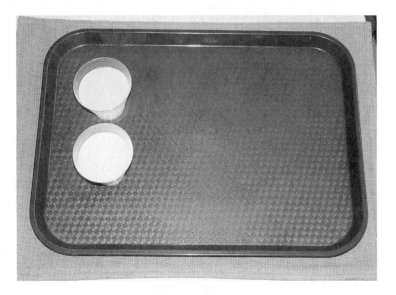

Nature Collection Tray Task

Materials

- one plastic rectangular tray
- a piece of solid color velvet or cloth fabric cut to fit tray
- shell or rock collection
- plastic wrapping
- magnifying glass

Setup

1. Place tray in horizontal position.
2. Place cloth on tray as background.
3. Arrange shell or rock collection on tray.
4. Cover collection with plastic wrapping.
5. Place magnifying glass to left of tray.

Task

Child views the collection through the magnifying glass, moving from left to right.

Outcome

Child uses observational skills when viewing nature collection while grasping magnifying glass.

Readiness Skills

Child is focusing eyes and hands and moving from left to right.

Safety Tip:

The plastic wrapping is for display purposes only and should not be handled by the children.

Nature Sorting Tray Task

 ## Materials

- one plastic rectangular tray
- collection of seashells, leaves, rocks, acorns, pinecones, feathers, and the like
- one cue written on sentence strip. For example:
    —series of dots from large to small
    —series of numbers

 ## Setup

1. Place tray in horizontal position.
2. Place collection on tray.
3. Place sentence strip across top of tray.

 ## Task

- Child is to look at cue strip and organize collection accordingly.

- Series of dots from large to small means to sort a row of the collection from largest to smallest.
- Series of numbers means to create columns under numbers with the correct amount of collection in each column.

 ## Outcome

Child successfully assigns a meaning to symbols and interprets them to complete the Tray Task.

 ## Readiness Skills

Child is using a skill necessary for encoding and decoding letter formations.

What Comes Next Tray Task

Materials

- ✖ one plastic rectangular tray
- ✖ three picture sets of three sequence science cards each
- ✖ basket

Setup

1. Place tray in horizontal position.
2. Place two sequence cards in a row on the tray.
3. Place remaining cards in basket to left of tray.

Task

■ Child is to look at the first two pictures of sequence.

 ■ Child is to select an ending picture that completes the sequence and place it in the correct order of events.

Outcome

Child successfully selects the appropriate ending sequence card and retells the series of events that are depicted.

Readiness Skills

This activity reinforces the concept of beginning, middle, and end as found in stories.

Used by permission from Carson Dellosa Publishing Company's CD-3120, Learning to Sequence: 3 Scene Set, CD 3116 First Words

CHAPTER 7

Family Notes

Families are a child's first teacher. They are our partner during a child's early years of growth and development. It is very important that we establish a chain of communication that is both meaningful and appropriate. Tray Tasking can deliver both of those essentials.

By using a Tray Tasking Observation Chart, we develop a tool for documenting a child's growth over time. Authentic assessment is achieved by observing children completing various Tray Tasks. We can visibly see the child's attempts and successes as the child builds confidence while engaged in Tray Tasks.

Many teachers provide families with daily notes, either individually or written about the entire class day. Families are very interested in knowing what topics we are covering, what skills their child is learning, and how their child is progressing. Tray Tasking is an important element in our ability to show families how children are learning the skills and concepts needed for kindergarten readiness.

The following opportunities are recommended to communicate that learning is occurring in the preschool classroom:

1. Always have Tray Tasks visible and on display.

2. Have a child demonstrate a new Tray Task at pickup time.

3. Copy and laminate the instruction page and display for viewing.

4. Demonstrate Tray Tasks at open houses, meetings, and conferences.

5. Start a manila file folder for each child that includes:

   a. Tray Task Observation Chart.

   b. other work you may wish to show family members, such as self-portraits, scissor cutting, drawings, dictated stories, photos, and the like.

6. Always date anything placed in the folder.

7. Share the child's folder at conferences, when the child is moving to the next classroom, or upon completion of a school year.

8. Send home a Tray Task Connection note when you are introducing a new Tray Task.

The following page contains a sample Tray Task Connection Note for Families. You can supply the name of the Tray Task.

Keep families informed of their child's progress, and they will build confidence in your ability to provide the very best environment of learning for their child. *Tray Tasking* provides meaningful and appropriate examples of kindergarten readiness activities.

Date: _____

Dear Family of _____:

Your child is preparing for formal reading and writing by completing our classroom Tray Tasks. This week we are emphasizing a task called:

_____.

All Tray Tasks are organized using two important directions that will be used for future reading and writing skills: top to bottom and left to right.

As your child reaches for an object on a tray, he or she is

- determining what hand to use.

- using the whole body in harmony through motion and movement.

- focusing the eyes to complete a task.

- crossing the midline of the body to promote left to right eye.

- tracking for future reading.

- strengthening arm, wrist, and finger muscles to hold a pencil.

All these skills are important ways we are observing that your child is getting ready for kindergarten.

Your child's teacher: _____

Tray Task
Observation Charts

The following pages contain a sample Tray Task Observation Chart, a blank Tray Task Observation Chart, and a blank Classroom Tray Task Observation Chart. There is no specified order to the Tray Tasks, so you can organize them around specific themes, holidays, or other unit focus topics. Remember that you can also substitute material within the Tray Task to be theme- or season-related. Modify and create your own Tray Tasks as long as you follow the left to right and top to bottom directionalities.

On the following pages are sample Tray Task Observation Charts. They are filled in for an individual child.

TRAY TASK OBSERVATION CHART

Date _____

Child's Name _____   Birth date _____

TRAY TASK	Good Job	With Teacher's Help	Not Yet	COMMENTS
1. Bead Tray Task				
2. Buckle				
3. Cloth Napkin Folding				
4. Clothes Folding				
5. Clothespin and Clothesline				
6. Cornmeal and Rice Sifter				
7. Dry Pouring				
8. Flower Arranging				
9. Hole Punch				
10. Lacing				
11. Ladle and Rice				
12. Large Button				
13. Mortar and Pestle				
14. Paper Tearing				

(continued)

TRAY TASK OBSERVATION CHART

Date _____

Child's Name _____   Birth date _____

TRAY TASK	Good Job	With Teacher's Help	Not Yet	COMMENTS
15. Pom-Pom and Tong				
16. Sand and Shell Sift				
17. Scoop and Beans				
18. Shape Sort				
19. Size Sort				
20. Snap Tray Task				
21. Spatula and Button				
22. Spoon and Grain				
23. Tire Tracks				
24. Tong and Button				
25. Tray Sweeping				
26. Tweezer Transfer				
27. Tying				
28. Zipper				

SAMPLE

TRAY TASK OBSERVATION CHART

Date _____

Child's Name _____   Birth date _____

TRAY TASK	Good Job	With Teacher's Help	Not Yet	COMMENTS
29. Baby Doll Wash				
30. Baster Transfer				
31. Bubble Beating				
32. Dish Washing				
33. Equal (Same As) Pouring				
34. Eyedropper				
35. Gelatin Squares				
36. Hand Washing				
37. Ice and Tong				
38. Measuring Liquid				
39. Mirror Washing				
40. Pipette				
41. Pouring and Measuring				
42. Sand and Water				

SAMPLE

(continued)

TRAY TASK OBSERVATION CHART

Date _____

Child's Name _____   Birth date _____

TRAY TASK	Good Job	With Teacher's Help	Not Yet	COMMENTS
43. Seashell Wash				
44. Sink and Float				
45. Small Cup with No Handles				
46. Small Pitcher with Handle				
47. Sponge Squeeze				
48. Spooning Liquid				
49. Syringe				
50. Table Washing				
51. Water Color Mixing				
52. Water Pouring				
53. Wire Whisk				
54. Addition				
55. Block				
56. Geoboard				

SAMPLE

TRAY TASK OBSERVATION CHART

Date _____

Child's Name _____   Birth date _____

TRAY TASK	Good Job	With Teacher's Help	Not Yet	COMMENTS
57. Lacing Cards				
58. Pegboard				
59. Pop Beads				
60. Puzzle				
61. Repeating Color (or Shape) Bead Pattern				
62. Small Blocks Stacking				
63. Take Away				
64. Blanket				
65. Lazy Eight				
66. Letter Forming				
67. Name				
68. Personalized				
69. Rhyming				
70. Straight Line Tracing				

(continued)

TRAY TASK OBSERVATION CHART

Date _____

Child's Name _____   Birth date _____

TRAY TASK	Good Job	With Teacher's Help	Not Yet	COMMENTS
71. Swirled Line Tracing				
72. Two-Handed Drawing				
73. Word Forming				
74. Applesauce				
75. Arrow				
76. Go Together				
77. Graduated				
78. Heavy to Light Weight				
79. Magnet Attraction				
80. Mixture Making				
81. Nature Collection				
82. Nature Sorting				
83. What Comes Next				

SAMPLE

On the following pages are blank Tray Task Observation Charts. They are for you to copy and use. Fill in the Tray Tasks you will be presenting. Copy and then label each page with the child's name and place in each child's file folder or loose-leaf notebook.

TRAY TASK OBSERVATION CHART

Date _____

Child's Name _____ Birth date _____

TRAY TASK	Good Job	With Teacher's Help	Not Yet	COMMENTS

TRAY TASK OBSERVATION CHART

Date _____

Child's Name _____   Birth date _____

TRAY TASK	Good Job	With Teacher's Help	Not Yet	COMMENTS

TRAY TASK OBSERVATION CHART

Date _____

Child's Name _____   Birth date _____

TRAY TASK	Good Job	With Teacher's Help	Not Yet	COMMENTS

TRAY TASK OBSERVATION CHART

Date _____

Child's Name _____   Birth date _____

TRAY TASK	Good Job	With Teacher's Help	Not Yet	COMMENTS

TRAY TASK OBSERVATION CHART

Date _____

Child's Name _____   Birth date _____

TRAY TASK	Good Job	With Teacher's Help	Not Yet	COMMENTS

On the following pages are sample observation charts for classroom use. Place the child's first name in the left column and insert the Tray Task across the top. Place the form on your clipboard and use it for anecdotal notes during the day. You can jot down more than one child's performance. You may then transfer your marks to the individual Tray Tasking Observation Chart at another time.

Use symbols to make your checking go faster:

   ✓   — Completed Task
WTH   — With Teacher's Help

Leave space blank if child could use another opportunity to succeed.

CLASSROOM TRAY TASK OBSERVATION CHART

TRAY TASKS →

CHILD'S NAMES ↓

1.						
2.						
3.						
4.						
5.						
6.						
7.						
8.						
9.						
10.						
11.						
12.						

CLASSROOM TRAY TASK OBSERVATION CHART

TRAY TASKS →							
CHILD'S NAMES ↓							
1.							
2.							
3.							
4.							
5.							
6.							
7.							
8.							
9.							
10.							
11.							
12.							

CLASSROOM TRAY TASK OBSERVATION CHART

TRAY TASKS →

CHILD'S NAMES ↓

1.							
2.							
3.							
4.							
5.							
6.							
7.							
8.							
9.							
10.							
11.							
12.							

CLASSROOM TRAY TASK OBSERVATION CHART

TRAY TASKS →							
CHILD'S NAMES ↓							
1.							
2.							
3.							
4.							
5.							
6.							
7.							
8.							
9.							
10.							
11.							
12.							

CLASSROOM TRAY TASK OBSERVATION CHART

	TRAY TASKS →						
CHILD'S NAMES ↓							
1.							
2.							
3.							
4.							
5.							
6.							
7.							
8.							
9.							
10.							
11.							
12.							

CLASSROOM TRAY TASK OBSERVATION CHART

	TRAY TASKS →						
CHILD'S NAMES ↓							
1.							
2.							
3.							
4.							
5.							
6.							
7.							
8.							
9.							
10.							
11.							
12.							

List of Materials

A

acorns

B

baskets
baster
bead pattern card showing six beads in alternating colors (or shapes)
beads of assorted colors (or shapes)
bins
black marker (write each child's name on a sentence strip twice)
blocks that connect
bowls (plastic and transparent; large and small)
brass fasteners
buttons

C

cinnamon sugar in shaker
clear bowl filled with water
clear gelatin mold
clear plastic cup
clear plastic drinking cups without handles
clear-gelled squares (made with clear gelatin mixture)
cloth napkin in solids bright colors
clothing items such as T-shirt and shorts
circle of solid color contact paper (5 inch)

colored pegs
colored pencils
colored rice
colored rubber bands
colored sand
containers
crayons
cue written on sentence strip
cup of colored rice or small beans
cup of sand
cup of water

D

diced wedges of apples (drop or two of lemon juice added)
dishcloth
dishtowel
dishwashing detergent
disposable paper towels
doll with an outfit that has a zipper
dried glue in the shape of a horizontal lazy eight figure on paper

F

feathers
food coloring
frame or doll with buttons on the outfit
frame or large shoe

frame with buckle belt or a stuffed doll with
    buckled belt

G

geoboard
glitter

H

hand towel
handheld flour sifter
handheld potato masher
handheld rotary eggbeater

I

ice cube tray
index cards showing an arrow on both cards
individual letters for simple three-letter words
individually cut letters for each child in individual
    envelopes with name printed on front

L

lace
laces attached to frame or shoelaces for shoes
lacing card
lacing string
laminated paper or plastic shapes
large colored pom-poms
large conch shell
large eyedropper
large metal or plastic tweezer
large plastic bin or bowl
large serving spoon
large shoe with two different colors of shoelaces
    knotted and laced through the shoe
large sponge
leaves
liquid dish detergent
liquid hand soap pump
liquid soap
liquid starch

M

magnet wand
magnifying glass
metal paper clips
mortar and pestle set

N

nailbrush or vegetable brush with handle
nature pictures of objects that either fly in the sky
    or swim in the ocean mounted on index cards

O

objects that sink and float

P

paint chip cards from hardware store of graduated
    shades and tints of three or four colors
paint placed in shallow bowl with blotter
pancake turner
paper confetti or sequins
paper cup
paper cut to fit inside tray
paper cut to fit over name strip
paper template of shapes in two rows of three
    shapes each
paper template of various size and shape outlines
    in two rows of three each
paper towels
pegboard
pegboard paper template strip
picture cards that rhyme with other picture cards
picture sets of three sequence science cards
pictures of three sets of items that go together
piece of solid color velvet or cloth fabric cut to fit
    tray
pinecones
pipette or slender eyedropper
plain paper cut to cover sentence strip name
plastic 2-cup measuring cup
plastic animals
plastic bowl filled with ice cubes
plastic circular tray
plastic coated paper clips in various colors
plastic cups
plastic dishes (assorted)
plastic drying rack
plastic flower vases
plastic flowers (three pairs)
plastic measuring cup of grain
plastic measuring cup of large uncooked beans
plastic or laminated paper shapes in various colors
plastic or wooden clothespins (spring type)
plastic pop beads
plastic measuring cup (1 cup)
plastic measuring cup with spouts and handles
    (2 cup)

plastic rectangular tray
plastic safety tong
plastic scoop
plastic spoon
plastic transparent bowls
plastic wrapping
plate
play dough or yarn
poster board cut to fit tray

R

rock collection
rocks
rubber spatula

S

safety tong
saltine crackers
sand
scraps of colored construction paper
seashells
section of clothesline
see-through plastic glasses
sentence strips with children's first names on them
sequins
serving spoon
set of large domino tiles or cards (teacher-made or
    store-bought)
shallow box
sheet of construction paper cut to fit tray
sheet of paper with continual two-inch swirled
    lines extending from left to right
sheet of paper with two-inch straight lines drawn
    from left to right
single hole paper punch
small nonpoisonous plant
small basket
small blocks in assortment of colors
small clothes bin (or lay clothes to side of tray)
small colorful plates
small container
small container of cornmeal

small handheld whisk broom with scoop
small pebble collection
small pictures (with no words) of word choices
small plastic bag
small plastic cup without handles
small plastic pitcher with a handle and a spout
small plastic plate
small safety mirror in a plastic frame
small sponge
small squirt bottle filled with soapy water
small suitcase with zipper or clasp for opening and
    closing
snap frame or doll with snap clothing
soap pump
solid color vinyl placemat fitted to length of tray or
    a tray with a column design
strings of yarn
strips of colored construction paper (1-inch x
    4-inch)
syringe

T

teacher-made cards showing numerals 1–5
tong
truck or car with rubber-tread wheels (small to
    medium size)

V

vinyl or laminated letter outlines
visual instruction card for sequencing of beads
    (store bought or teacher made)

W

washable doll
washcloth
water
water with added liquid color or food coloring
watering can with spout and handle filled with
    water
white glue
wire whisk
wooden puzzle in frame

Readiness Skills Index

A

assigning meaning to materials, 7
attention to task, 41
auditory discrimination, 74

C

causes hands to work together to achieve success, 67
centering attention toward the center of the body, 20
completion of a task, 10, 12, 22, 38
concentration skills, 89
connecting oral and written language, 77
control of arm, wrist, and finger movement, 44, 53, 70
coordinate body motions, 13, 40, 65
coordinates body actions and eyes, 14
coordinates movement of both hands and arms, 52
coordinating body balance and movement, 22
coordination of body movement, 44, 58
crossing the midline, 9, 8, 13, 14, 16, 21, 23, 27, 28, 30, 36, 40, 44, 49, 50, 51, 52, 53, 58, 59, 68, 70, 86, 87, 88, 89

D

determines which hand to use, 59

E

encoding and decoding letter formations, 94
encourage coordinated movements to achieve a goal, 9
encourage following of directions, 10
eye tracking, 8, 62, 63, 81, 89
eye-hand coordination, 8, 11, 12, 15, 16, 19, 21, 24, 25, 26, 27, 30, 32, 36, 38, 41, 45, 50, 53, 57, 64, 70, 81, 82, 86, 88, 89

F

fine motor skills, 26, 41, 64
fine muscle development, 8, 16, 32, 38, 47
focus while strengthening arm and hand muscles, 86
focuses eyes and hands toward the middle of the midline, 34, 67
focusing body to center of midline, 64
focusing eyes, hand/arm movements toward the center of the body, 20
following directions, 26
forms simple three-letter words, 83

G

grasping and coordinating movements, 18, 21, 22, 23, 28, 29, 32, 45, 50, 54, 81

Web Resources

Listed here are several suggested Web sites for additional resources and ideas:

<http://www.theideabox.com>   This is an early childhood education and activity resource provided by the National Child Care Information Center (NCCIC).

<http://www.earlychildhood.com>   This early childhood resource Web site is provided by Discount School Supply.

<http://www.discountschoolsupply.com>   This is the Web site of a school supply company for early childhood centers and schools.

<http://www.smarterkids.com>   This Web site is about educational toys for parents and families.

<http://www.preksmarties.com>   This preschool education resource for parents teaching preschoolers provides tips for early reading, parenting activities, family freebies, and the like.

<http://prek.dhs.org>   PreK central provides creative activities just for preschoolers.

<http://www.educationworld.com>   This is an early childhood resource for teachers and parents.

<http://www.bambini-montessori.com>   This Montessori Web site provides products. Click Pre List and then click Practical Life.

Tray Tasking Tips and Guidelines for Classroom Success

When you set up your Tray Tasking trays, remember these guidelines:

1. Look for colorful, color-coordinated materials.

2. Select items that are childproof by checking for soft edges and easy-to-grasp sizes.

3. Use plastic and wooden materials rather than glass.

4. Local party stores are a good resource for trays and transferring items.

5. Display at least 10 tray tasks in a learning center.

6. Rotate your tray tasks as you see children accomplish their goals. This is usually every six weeks.

7. Place tray tasks in their own learning center if possible. Emphasize that the materials remain on the tray and are not used for other learning center activities.

8. Take pictures of children working with and completing Tray Tasks. Create a Parent Information Board displaying pictures with short explanations below.

9. Emphasize to parents that the Tray Tasks are preparing children for reading and writing skills.

10. Always label shelving with Tray Task name and a picture of task. This way children will place task tray back when finished.

"Reading and Writing" Fun in the Kitchen!

The following article is written for families who might wish to explore ways to create learning tasks at home. Please feel free to copy and distribute it to your families or use in a newsletter. If you or the families of your children have questions, you can contact me at <u>vfolds@msn.com</u>.

Everything a child does is an adventure toward learning something new or revisiting something learned. Exploring and investigating the world around them fascinates young children. One of the first places for learning to take place is in the home. Your home provides wonderful opportunities for young children to learn about their environment. Let's focus on some specific tips for you as parents and family that will help you see that activities and tasks you are already doing at home are equipping your children for the learning mode.

Every room in your home provides tools for reading and writing skills to be developed. Young children need opportunities to exercise and use their large and small muscles, coordinate eyes and hands to work together, and use the whole body when refining movements that will grow into reading and writing skills.

Did you know that when you recite Patty-Cake as your infant sits in your lap and you place your hands on the infant's hands as your clap together,

you are preparing the body for reading and writing? By clapping hands together, a child is meeting the midline of the body. The midline is an imaginary line down the center of the body that promotes coordination as a child grows and matures. As children use motions that cross the midline (swaying arms back and forth in front of their body, using both hands to hold a broom or bat a ball), the eyes are focusing and strengthening. The body is working in harmony to achieve a positive result.

Families are always concerned about their child reading and writing at an early age. The formal reading and writing will come after the child has had sufficient opportunities to refine the midline, strengthen movements, increase small motor muscle abilities, and coordinate eyes and hands movements. These movements and abilities are happening right before your eyes, in your own home. Everyday chores, tasks, and activities that you do with your child are naturally allowing the body to get ready to read and write.

The following activities involve motions and movements that prepare your child for kindergarten. The focus is on the fascination children have with the kitchen. Here are some ideas to create fun experiences in the kitchen as your child learns to coordinate muscles, refine eye and hand strengths, and spend time with you in meaningful, fun ways. You can refer to these activities as learning tasks as you encourage your child to join you in the kitchen!

KITCHEN LEARNING ACTIVITIES

When preparing meals, provide a child-safe area where your child can perform tasks similar to what you are doing.

- If you are mixing batter, place a small amount in a child-safe bowl and provide a whisk or large spoon. This encourages small muscle control and eye-hand coordination, both of which your child will use when reading and writing. The stirring motion crosses the midline. In order for two eyes and two arms and two hands to function properly, they must work in harmony, so crossing the midline increases the ability to work together. You will also notice which hand holds the spoon, which gives you a hint as to your child's handedness (whether your child will be right- or left-handed).

- Canned goods organization: Encourage your preschooler to help stock the shelves. This activity provides plenty of practice in classifying by type (all soups go here, all vegetables go there), or by size (put all tall cans in the back, short jars in the front), or by name. I have been in some kitchens where the shelf contents are organized alphabetically!

- Silverware drawers: Encourage your preschooler to place the silverware in the proper places. Usually people have the separated organizers in the drawers that may be molded to indicate the type of utensil to place in it.

Your child can also empty the drawer and set the table for dinner. This activity will encourage one-to-one correspondence (we need three forks: one for mommy, one for sister, and one for me, etc.)

- Coupons: Encourage your preschooler to place your coupons for the next shopping trip in order by types of foods. While grocery shopping, your preschooler could help select foods according to the pictures on the coupons. This encourages a reading technique called sight recognition. Your child applies a symbol to a meaning and makes a connection between a picture and a real object or words to words.

- Flouring a baking pan: Lightly grease the bottom of a shallow baking pan and gently sprinkle with flour. Encourage your preschooler to draw or write with his or her finger in the flour. You can also use cornmeal. This is a great writing time activity.

- Water transfer: Place two different types of measuring cups on a tray. A two-cup and a one-cup work well. Fill one with a little water and encourage your preschooler to pour from one to another. Remember to place the filled one on the left so that your child can practice left to right progression. This might lead to using a creamer-type dispenser at the dinner table filled with a beverage so that your preschooler can pour his or her own drink. This encourages eye-hand coordination and grasping practice and increases self-esteem because you are saying "Good job" as your child successfully attempts the task.

A preschooler is always a willing partner when you are in the kitchen. The activities that you do together provide a special one-on-one time with your preschooler. Your child will also be calmer because these types of activities are fun and require lots of concentration.

Enjoy these suggestions as you and your child read and write in the kitchen!

Easy Tools for Early Learning

Maria Montessori tells us in *Dr. Montesori's Own Handbook* (1914) that there are two functions that must be established by the young child in order for his or her intelligence to have continual exercise in observation, comparison, and judgment: "motor functions by which he is to secure his balance and learn to walk and to coordinate his movement" and "the sensory functions through which, receiving sensations from his environment, the child lays a foundation for learning."

These two functions, motor and sensory, provide the stimulation needed for active learning to occur. As adults, whether family member or teacher, basic presentation techniques are recommended so that children are not only receiving new information from the adult (Piaget's assimilation theory), they are also making sense of the new information (Piaget's accommodation theory). Montessori's way of presenting new knowledge to young children is through her three-period lesson. This presentation technique is a quick, easy way to promote motor and sensory stimulation.

Period 1: **Naming**—provide a name for the object or concept you are sharing with a child. Use these words: "This is . . . ."

Period 2: **Recognition**—ask the child to choose, from several objects, the one you have named. Use these words: "Show me the . . . ."

Period 3: **The Pronunciation of the Word(s)**—now ask the child to verbalize the object you are presenting. Use these words: "What is this?"

In short, we remember them as the "this is, show me, and what is" method.

This method can be applied to Tray Tasking tasks as well.

1. When demonstrating a Tray Task to students, begin with explaining the task: "This is the Baster Transfer Tray Task."

2. When a child chooses to complete the Baster Transfer Tray Task, the adult can then ask the child to look at the Tray Task and discriminate among the objects on the tray when the adult suggests, "Show me the baster."

3. To continue the learning process, the adult can then point to the Tray Task and ask, "What is this?" so that the child can verbalize the name of the Tray Task.

In the first two period presentations, the child is assimilating or absorbing the information, in the last period presentation, the child is actively engaged in confirming the acquisition of the knowledge by recognizing the object and using its name. Thus, accommodation has occurred so that the child reproduces the new information through speaking. Tray Tasking can take on a new dimension when you incorporate this type of inquiry into your observation and documentation.

I have found that this type of approach works with the majority of information that I am sharing with young children. I use this technique with one child or a small group.

Let's say, for example, that you are introducing a shape to a child. Research tells us that children learn through touch first, and then sight. Thus, we offer learning through the manipulation of hands-on materials that can be touched and seen in order for learning to take place.

Let's set up the three-period lesson with shape awareness in mind.

Period 1: **Naming**—provide a name for the shape you are showing a child. Use these words: "This is a circle."

Period 2: **Recognition**—ask the child to choose, from several shapes, the one you have named. Use these words: "Show me the circle."

Period 3: **The Pronunciation of the Word(s)**—now ask the child to verbalize the circle shape you are presenting. Use these words: "What is this?"

When the child provides the correct response, you have assurance that a cycle of learning has occurred. This cycle of learning may need reinforcement and repetition, but you have begun the journey toward the child's ability to recall and remember.

If the child provides an incorrect response, you have an opportunity to repeat the three-period lesson. This is not failure on the child's part, but an indication to the adult that a cycle of learning did not begin. The adult might wish to explore other ways to present the lesson. Rather than use a one-dimensional shape, the adult might have a shape hunt or other such physical activity to stimulate the child.

Integrating your concept of the day throughout your learning centers is a recommended approach. If your objective is to help children learn shapes that day or week, think of all the opportunities you have in your environment for reinforcement of that objective to take place. Plan events in each of your learning centers that reflect that shape. For example: If a circle shape is a concept goal, then target areas where circles are found. In your Block Area, ask children to gather all cylinder shapes or objects that have no corners. Have the children bring them to the carpet for discussion. You can then sort and discuss each selection and whether it fits the criteria to be a circle shape. In the Language area, you can find all felt letters for the flannel board that are circular in shape. In the Math area, you can ask children to find all counters that are circle shaped. In the Small Manipulative area, collect all small connectors that are circle shaped.

Bring all these objects to the carpet. The adult produces a large hoop and places it on the floor. Each child is to select one circle shape from the collection and place it in the hoop. The teacher produces another hoop and places it next to the first hoop. Now ask the children to choose only from the shapes in the hoop. Ask for another attribute or characteristic such as color or size or thickness. These selections become part of the second hoop. We are sorting and classifying, and children are using tactile and visual discrimination in decision-making.

Another activity would be to label objects in the room that are circle shaped. The adult could have precut circles and a bold marker and write the word *circle* on each one. Children then adhere the circle label to objects in the classroom that are circle shaped. I would also suggest that you serve circle crackers at snack time. Provide circle cookie cutters and have children cut cheese slices into circle shapes to place on their crackers. What a great way to infuse the shape concept throughout the learning center areas.

You can take any concept you wish to teach, use the three-period lesson, and prepare the learning environment to highlight the concept. Your classroom will take on a new purpose to the children every time you emphasize a new concept.

Sources

Montessori, Maria. (1965). *Dr. Montessori's Own Handbook*. New York: Schocken Books.

Piaget, J. (1962). *Play, dreams, and imitation in children*. New York: Norton.